SERMON STARTERS FROM
THE GREEK NEW TESTAMENT

Sermon Starters
from the
GREEK
NEW
TESTAMENT

Gerald Cowen

BROADMAN PRESS

Nashville, Tennessee

All Scripture references are from the King James Version or the author's own translation of the Greek text.

Dewey Decimal Classification: 251.01
Subject heading: **SERMONS - OUTLINES, SYLLABI, ETC.**
Library of Congress Catalog Card Number: 84-27448
Printed in the United States of America

Library of Congress Cataloging in Publication Data

Cowen, Gerald, 1942-
    Sermon starters from the Greek New Testament.

    Bibliography: p.
    Includes index.
    1. Greek language, Biblical—Terms and phrases.
2. Bible. N.T.—Language, style. 3. Preaching.
4. Theology—Terminology. I. Title.
PA875.C69 1985   487'.4   84-27488
ISBN 0-8054-1397-9 (pbk.)

DEDICATION

*To my wife Mary
my fellowlaborer
in the gospel*

Foreword

Since my days in the Southern Baptist Theological Seminary, the study of the Greek New Testament has had special significance for me. The preacher's ability to make use of insights gained from studying the text and the language of its authors can provide remarkable understanding for the parishioners who will hear that pastor. However, the task must be skillfully done; otherwise, the preacher will appear to be pedantic, ostentatious, or worse.

Therefore, the preacher who wishes to be a skilled expositor of the Word of God will welcome this book by Dr. Gerald Cowen, our esteemed professor of New Testament and Greek here at the Criswell Center for Biblical Studies. Not only is Dr. Cowen a skilled expositor of the Word, but he also directs our Encounter Missions Division at the Criswell Center which was responsible this past year for the conversions of nearly 4,000 people.

As you read these remarkable word studies, you will discover in them that great evangelical confluence of the warm heart and the sharpened mind. May they be as much of a blessing to you as they have been to me.

W. A. CRISWELL
Pastor's Study
First Baptist Church, Dallas

Preface

Many who have preceded us have labored to understand and explain more clearly the use of certain words and phrases in the New Testament. One of those, Kenneth Wuest, has correctly written, "One who undertakes to study God's Word and to explain it to others, should be a student of words. To the extent that he understands the meaning of the words in the New Testament, to that extent is he able to understand its statements and make them clear to others."

The words of the New Testament are the building blocks of Christian theology, and "he who will not begin with a patient study of those, shall never make any considerable, least of all any secure, advances in this: for here, as everywhere else, some disappointment awaits him who thinks to possess the whole without first possessing the parts of which that whole is composed" (Trench).

The Greek language of the New Testament is rich indeed, and there are sometimes subtle distinctions between words which are similar in meaning. One who desires to know God's word to the fullest degree will wish to search out these distinctions, which are often passed over by the casual reader, for it is these words which convey the thought and meaning of the author. It is important that we do not miss the intention of the author because we did not understand the more basic elements—the words. When we are dealing with the Word of God it is, as Trench points out, "desirable that we should miss nothing" because these words of Scripture are "the vehicles of the very mind of God Himself."

The purpose of this small volume is to open up to the pastor or layperson, who either does not know Greek or has a somewhat limited knowledge of it, some of the depth and richness found in the vocabulary of the New Testament. It is hoped that this will give the reader insight into the text, which would have been missed in reading the English text alone, and that these new insights will inspire the reader to a deeper study of the Word of God and a more fruitful ministry for the Lord.

The intention of the author has not been to give a complete listing of every word's appearance in the New Testament. For that information, one should consult a work such as *Strong's Exhaustive Concordance.* However, references for some words, which occur a limited number of times, are fully listed.

The main emphasis has been to survey the use of a word in secular literature and Jewish sources, such as the Septuagint translation of the Old Testament, to see if there is any information there which will shed light on how the word should be translated and interpreted in the New Testament. An effort has been made to organize the material, when possible, so it may be more readily used by the reader for sermons and devotional purposes.

The English translation generally used in this volume is the King James Version. However, in some cases the author's own revision of that translation is used.

GERALD COWEN
Dallas, Texas

Contents

1

Peace

Eirene (peace) seems to be derived from the verb *eiro*, which means to join or to speak or to converse with someone. So, in its basic meaning, peace describes a state in which people are joined together rather than being alienated from each other; they are on friendly, speaking terms with each other.

Eirene is a most common word in the New Testament; it appears in every book except 1 John. Moreover, it has a variety of usages. It may refer to: (1) safety and security (freedom from danger—In Luke 19:42, Jesus speaks concerning Jerusalem and the peace which it had in that day, but warns that it will end); (2) harmony between nations, or the lack of war (Rev. 6:4, the rider of the red horse was given power to take peace from the earth); (3) harmony between individuals (Matt. 10:34 contrasts peace with the strife that will come because of the gospel); and (4) order, which is the opposite of confusion, either in the state (Acts 24:2) or in the church (1 Cor. 14:33).

(5) In addition, *Eirene* is commonly used as a greeting which corresponds to the Hebrew word *shalom* (peace be unto you), and also as a blessing such as: "go in peace" (1 Cor. 16:11). (6) However, the greatest use of the word is to represent the rest and contentment one has as a result of a harmonious relationship with God, which is a result of the gospel of Jesus Christ (Acts 10:36; Rom. 5:1).

In the Hebrew mind, peace is sometimes equated with salvation. The Greek Old Testament (Septuagint) translates the phrase for "peace offering" (Lev. 3:1) as "salvation-offering." One of the titles for God in the New Testament is the "God of peace" (Rom. 15:33; Phil. 4:9), which means that our God is One who brings salvation, order, harmony, and security to our lives.

2
Prayer

In Philippians 1:3-4, two words are used to describe different types of prayer: *eucharisteō* (I give thanks) and *deesis* (prayer, request). *Deesis,* which is used twice in verse four, usually refers to requests made by men to God (James 5:16; Acts 1:14), although it also may be directed to men. More specifically, it is an entreaty or a supplication to God for some matter of personal need; it is a prayer for particular benefits (Phil. 1:19; Luke 1:13). Therefore, in Ephesians 6:18, where *deesis* is used, we are encouraged to pray for *specific* needs: "Praying always with all prayer and supplication [*deesis*] in the Spirit."

Eucharisteō, on the other hand, means: (1) to feel grateful or thankful (Rom. 16:4); (2) to give thanks for something (1 Thess. 2:13); or (3) to consecrate a thing by giving thanks for it (Justin, *Apology* 1. 65-66). Its most frequent use is to denote a prayer of thanksgiving to God (Phil. 4:6), and as such it is essentially a word of praise, for we praise God by the "grateful acknowledgement of past mercies." It will exist in heaven (Rev. 4:9; 7:12) in a fuller manner, "for only there will the redeemed know how much they owe to their Lord; and this it will do, while all other forms of prayer, in the very nature of things, will have ceased in the entire possession and present fruition of the things prayed for" (Trench).

Two additional words for prayer are used in conjunction with the two already mentioned in 1 Timothy 2:1. Paul exhorts Timothy not only to give thanks (*eucharisteō*) and make supplication (*deesis*) for all men, but he includes prayer (*proseuche*) and petition (*en-*

teuxis) for all men as well. *Proseuche* denotes prayer in general and is a word that is "restricted to sacred uses; it is always prayer to God" (Trench).

Enteuxis, on the other hand, is a much more specific word, although in its only other appearance in the New Testament it is also translated by the same general word that *proseuche* is: "prayer" (1 Tim. 4:5). It does not mean intercession in relation to others in the present sense of the word. A different picture is at the heart of it. The verb form (*entugchanein*) originally represented the idea of meeting a person and getting close to him in order to converse and even to have intimate fellowship with that person. This idea is bound up in *enteuxis.*

Barclay cites the story of Thaues and Taous, who served at the Temple of Serapis in Memphis, Egypt. When Ptolemy Philometer and Cleopatra visited the temple, they seized the opportunity to present the king a petition (*enteuxis*) for justice. It is the word for a petition to the king. Its fundamental idea includes freedom of access to present such a petition. The Christian believer has the privilege of access to present his petitions to the King of kings. Let us not forget that "prayer is nothing less than entering into the presence of the Almighty and receiving the resources of the Eternal" (Barclay).[1]

3

Grace

Charis (grace) is an example of a word which was adopted by Christian writers. They magnified it to reveal its greatest and highest meaning. In the Greek Old Testament it signifies something which gives joy or pleasure to those who hear or see it, such as graciousness or beauty of speech (Eccl. 10:12). In the New Testament, it is used in reference to the "gracious words" Jesus spoke at the synagogue in His hometown of Nazareth (Luke 4:22). Grace itself was embodied or contained in that gracious act.

Its meaning later was extended to denote the act itself, such as a favor someone might grant to another (the kindness of a master toward his servants—Luke 1:30). Finally, it also began to signify thanks or gratitude to someone for a gracious act: "Does he *thank* that servant because he did the things that were commanded him?" (Luke 17:9, see also Heb. 12:28).

From the time of Paul, the word was uplifted to denote a heavenly rather than an earthly benefit; he uses it in reference to God's favor and kindness to men (Acts 7:46). It indicates "a favour freely done, without claim or expectation of return" (Trench). Its only motive is the kindness of the giver. Paul demonstrates this when he contrasts grace to works (Rom. 4). Examples of undeserved blessings God's grace has bestowed on mankind are: salvation (Eph. 2:8-9) and grace (spiritual) gifts to believers (Rom. 12:6, Eph. 4:7).

Three aspects of grace are outlined in the New Testament. (1) Not only is the favor which God has bestowed upon us through

17

His gracious acts emphasized, but (2) God's "friendly disposition from which the kindly act proceeds, graciousness, lovingkindness, goodwill" (Vine) is also evident (Acts 14:26). Finally, (3) there is the result of grace, the state of those who have experienced it.

This meaning is found in the Epistle to the Romans: "By whom we have access by faith into this grace wherein we stand, and rejoice in hope of the glory of God" (Rom. 5:2).

4

Be Ye Holy

The term *hagios* (holy), which is found in many New Testament passages, is used in three different respects. (1) It is used to describe God—He is holy or worthy of reverence. Luke 1:49 says of Him, "He that is mighty hath done to me great things, and holy is His name." (2) *Hagios* also refers to "things which on account of some connection with God possess a certain distinction and claim to reverence"; these things are sacred and not to be profaned (Thayer), such as the temple (Matt. 24:15), the holy city (Matt. 4:5), the covenant (Luke 1:72), and the Scriptures (Rom. 1:2). (3) The most important use of this term is to describe those persons who are set apart exclusively for God. Examples are the apostles (Eph. 3:5), the prophets (Acts 3:21), and the angels (Mark 8:38).

In addition to these special groups, the New Testament applies this word to the partakers of salvation (1 Peter 2:9). Paul says, "For the unbelieving husband is sanctified [verb form of the same word] by the wife . . . otherwise your children would be unclean, but now are they *holy*" (1 Cor. 7:14). Again, Paul says of the Gentiles, "For if the first fruit is holy, the batch is also holy, and if the root is holy, so are the branches" (Rom. 11:16). All believers are to live lives which are in "glaring contrast with the impurity and sensuality of the Gentiles" (H. A. A. Kennedy). They are to be holy in heart and conduct (1 Pet. 1:16).

The root idea in holiness is *purity*. The believer is to keep himself clean and pure for the Lord's service. The plural of this term, *hagioi,* is translated "holy ones" or "saints" (Phil. 1:1), and the verb form (*hagiazō*) is translated "to sanctify" (1 Cor. 7:14).

5

The Lord's Slave

In Titus 1:1, Paul says that he is a *doulos* of Jesus Christ. Prior to, and even during New Testament times, this word referred to a "slave." *Doulos* denoted "one that is in a permanent relation of servitude to another, his will altogether swallowed up in the will of the other" who is his master or Lord (Trench). More specifically, it signified one who was a born bondman or slave in contrast to an *andrapoden,* one who was captured or sold into slavery (Liddell and Scott).

In the New Testament, *doulos* is most often translated by the word "servant." The apostles, for instance, are called "servants" of the church for Jesus' sake (2 Cor. 4:5). However, the term "servant" is somewhat misleading. A servant is one who performs services for someone else, but the term does not indicate whether the one who performs these services is a free man or a slave. In secular Greek, a *doulos* is one who serves because of his servile relationship to a master. In the first-century world, the *doulos* occupied the lowest servile position in society.

The New Testament employs this term to show the sinner's relationship to sin. Jesus said, "Whosoever committeth sin is the servant of sin" (John 8:34). After the bondage to sin is ended, *doulos* is then used to describe the believer's new relationship to God. Believers are not merely to be servants, but devoted slaves to Jesus Christ (Acts 4:29). In the truest sense of the word, believers have not been sold into slavery but have been born into the service of Christ by the new birth (Rom. 6:16-18). In this latter case, however, "the servility and abjectness are not included in the meaning of the word, but the fact that the Bible writers used it to describe the Christian, shows that they desired to retain its connotation of humbleness" (Wuest).

6
Sin

The concept of sin "may be regarded under an infinite number of aspects, and in all languages has been so regarded; and as the diagnosis of it belongs most of all to the Scriptures, nowhere else are we likely to find it contemplated on so many sides" (Trench). In fact, there are seven words in the New Testament which describe various aspects of this concept. The principal word used for sin is *hamartia*. The origin of the word is uncertain and has been a matter of debate among scholars; it is certain, however, that *hamartia* refers to "missing the mark," or a failure to attain the goal God has set for us. The Greek poet Homer uses the word to describe the soldier who hurls his spear but fails to strike his foe (*Iliad* 4. 491) Thucydides, in his *History of the Peloponnesian War,* utilized it to describe soldiers who missed the road they were to take and therefore perished at the hand of the enemy (3. 98.2).

From these usages, the word was next applied to intellectual persuits. Aristotle spoke of a poet who "sins" by selecting a subject which is beyond his ability to describe (*Poetics* 8 and 25). This use has no ethical import, however; it is only a mistake. According to Trench, Plato was the only pagan writer who used it in an ethical sense similar to its use in the New Testament (*Republic* 2. 366A).

In the New Testament, *hamartia* is the opposite of "righteousness" (conformity to the standard set by God). It is pictured from three standpoints. (1) It is a principle or source of mankind's actions (the inward element which produces acts—W.E. Vine; Rom. 3:9; 5:12). (2) It is described as a power exercising dominion.

Romans 6:12 says, "Let not sin therefore reign in your mortal body"; Romans 6:14 adds, "For sin shall not lord it over you."

(3) Finally, it refers to "that which is done wrong." It may be something committed in thought, speech, or action (see Matt. 5:22,28); it may be something necessary which was omitted (see Matt. 23:23); or it may be an action which produced a particular result (James 1:15). The word may refer to sin generally (John 8:46), sin collectively (John 1:29), or some specific deed (Acts 7:60).

However, a specific act of sin is also denoted by the sister word, *hamartema*. In all these instances it refers to violation of God's law: "Sin is the transgression of the law" (1 John 3:4).

7

Sin, Sin, and More Sin

As mentioned before There are seven basic words which describe the concept of sin, and many others are used occasionally
to express what we call "sin." Two of these—*hamartia* (missing the
mark) and *hamartema* (an act of missing the mark)—have been
discussed in the previous section. The remaining five words will be
considered together.

First, there is *asebeia* (ungodliness), which denotes a lack of
reverence toward God. It may refer to: impiety in general (Rom.
1:18; 11:26; Tit. 2:12), specific deeds (Jude 15), or ungodly desires
(Jude 18). Trench describes *asebeia* as "active irreligion." It is "a
deliberate withholding from God of His dues of prayer and of
service, a standing, so to speak, in a battle array against Him." In
the Old Testament, the *asebes* (ungodly man) set himself in opposition to the righteous man, who did the will of God (Gen. 18:23).

A second word is *parakoe,* which is usually translated
"disobedience." Literally, it means "hearing amiss." It may be
used in reference to (1) the act of neglect in the matter of hearing,
(2) carelessness in listening, or (3) the overt refusal to hear
(disobedience). It is found in opposition to *hupakoe* (obedience) in
Romans 5:19, 2 Corinthians 10:6, and Hebrews 2:2.

In the New Testament, the verb form of the word is found
only in Matthew 18:17, where it clearly means "to refuse to hear."
The refusal to hear seems to follow after carelessness in hearing the
message of God, or as Trench puts it, "The sin may be regarded
as already committed in the failing to listen when God is speak-

ing." An Old Testament example of this is found in Adam, who was careless about listening to God; this carelessness was a sign of his inward attitude toward God's command which led to his act of disobedience. In the fullest sense, the lack of earnest attempt to know God's will is sin (Wuest). (See also Jer. 11:10, 35:17).

The third type of sin is *anomia* (without law or lawlessness). In the New Testament, it is most often translated "iniquity" (Matt. 7:23; Rom. 6:19; 2 Cor. 6:14; Heb. 10:17; 1 John 3:4). In classical Greek, it is used in connection with *anarchia,* which refers to a people without government (anarchy). One who does not accept government is lawless (Wuest). In the New Testament, *anomia* does not denote the condition of one who is living without law, but "the condition or deed of one who acts contrary to the law" (Trench). It describes one who has contempt for Divine law (2 Thess. 2:3,7), one who is opposed to righteousness (2 Cor. 6:14). In Romans 2:14, the Gentiles could be charged with sin (*adikia* —unrighteousness—or *hamartia*—missing the mark), but not with *anomia,* because the law had not yet been given to them. However, before the law of Moses, all were still sinners.

A fourth word related to the concept of sin is *parabasis,* a going aside, an overstepping, a transgression. In order to be a transgressor, there must first be a boundary to transgress. Romans 5:14 is a good example of this truth: "but death reigned from Adam until Moses even upon the ones who did not sin (*hamartia*) after the likeness of Adam's sin" (*parabasis*). In Roman literature it was described as an act which is excessive and more serious than *hamartia* (Cicero, *Paradoxa* 3). As Trench points out: after the law was given, people could no longer just be sinners, but transgressors also. *Parabasis* is used in Romans 2:23, 4:15, and 5:14; Galatians 3:19; 1 Timothy 2:14; and Hebrews 2:2 and 9:15.

The final word included in this discussion of New Testament words describing sin is *paraptoma,* which is usually translated as "a fault." In Greek literature it refers to a false step or blunder, a defect, or a transgression. It is used by the Greek writer, Longinus, to describe literary faults. In the New Testament, it is sometimes employed as a synonym of *parabasis* (transgression of a known rule of life—Wuest); it is a deviation from righteousness and truth (see Matt. 6:14-15).

In contrast, however, *paraptoma* is not as strong a word as *parabasis*. It may also refer to an error in judgment or other fault (Gal. 6:1). As Trench puts it, *paraptoma* is sometimes used "to designate sins not of the deepest dye and the worst enormity." It may refer to a sin caused by ignorance of "what one ought to have known." Yet one should not make the mistake of taking it lightly because it is still pictured as serious and deadly. It is the cause of spiritual death (Eph. 2:1) and the fall of Israel (Rom. 11:11-12).

In conclusion, sin is described in the New Testament as:

(1) missing the mark (*hamartia*)
(2) an evil deed (*hamartema*)
(3) ungodliness (*asebeia*)
(4) disobedience—refusal to hear (*parakoe*)
(5) lawlessness (*anomia*)
(6) transgression (*parabasis*)
(7) a blunder (*paraptoma*).

Each of these words describes a different aspect of what sin is. Though they are not the same, they are all wrong and cause us to be guilty before God.

8

Fellowship

In secular Greek documents, the word *koinonía* (fellowship) has three distinct meanings. (1) It is commonly used to describe business partnerships. (2) It speaks of the closest of all human relationships, marriage. *Koinonía* is found in marriage contracts in the time of Augustus Caesar (Moulton and Milligan). (3) The classical writer Epictetus used the term in the context of having "fellowship with Zeus" (*Discourses* 2. 19.27).

Moreover, believers are specifically commanded not to have "fellowship with [participate in] the unfruitful works of darkness, but rather, reprove them (Eph. 5:11, verb form). This would apply to a business partnership with unbelievers or participation in the worship of false gods. In addition, the believer is not to share in the evil deeds of someone else or shelter a law breaker.

On the positive side, the verb form of the word, *koinoneō,* describes the beautiful relationship that marriage should be. In classical Greek times, a doctor put up a monument to his deceased wife which read, "I *shared* all life with you alone" (Barclay).[2]

Koinonía is translated several different ways in the New Testament. Some of its meanings are fellowship, communion, contribution, distribution, and communication. The primary idea expressed is a fellowship which is based on an "intimate association, a close relationship" (Acts 2:42; Gal. 2:9; 1 John 1:3). As such, it often referred to the marital relationship in Greek literature.

A second use of *koinonía* is to describe a "joint participation or sharing in something, a partnership." Paul wanted to "participate" in the sufferings of Christ (Phil. 3:10). Believers have a "joint participation" in the blood of Christ (1 Cor. 10:16).

A third meaning of *koinonía* is a "contribution or gift" (jointly donated) which is a sign of fellowship. The Christians of Macedonia and Achaia sent a gift for the poor at Jerusalem (Rom. 15:26).

Believers have a fellowship among themselves which they cannot have with the world because: (1) they have a close relationship with Christ and His body, the church, and (2) they have a joint participation in something (the atoning blood of Christ) which they do not have in common with unbelievers.

9

Unequally Yoked

In 2 Corinthians 6:14, the apostle Paul gives a command to his fellow Christians: "Do not become unequally yoked with unbelievers." The focal word in this command is *heterozugeo,* which means to yoke unequally or to yoke with another of a different sort.

This verb is not found anywhere else in Scripture, although the same word in adjective form is found in the Greek version of Leviticus 19:19 concerning the different kinds of animals. Paul's reference undoubtedly recalls the reference in Deuteronomy 22:10, which says, "Thou shalt not plough with an ox and an ass together." Liddell and Scott cite the use of the noun form of the word in grammar to indicate words "differently declined." Believers and unbelievers certainly belong to a different family with an entirely different set of values.

In what regard are unbelievers and believers to avoid being "yoked" or bound together? While the word *heterozugeō* does not specify any particular relationship, some of the other words used in the same passage offer an answer (2 Cor. 6:14ff.). Following this command, there is a series of five rhetorical questions which make us see the folly of such a union. In the first question, "What fellowship has righteousness with unrighteousness?" the key word in the question is fellowship (*metoche*). The idea expressed by *metoche* is a "sharing or partnership." A first century papyrus receipt uses a form of the word to describe a man named "Sotas and his *associates*" (business partners), who were "collectors of money-taxes." The primary use of this word in secular literature is to denote business partnerships (see Moulton and Milligan).

The second question Paul asks, which is related to the yoking of unequal partners, is "What communion (*koinonía*) has light with darkness?" The obvious answer is *none.* While *koinonía* has already been discussed in the preceding study, let us note that it is often used in connection with business partnerships in the same manner as *metoche.* However, *koinonía* is a more intense word and is often used relative to the closest human relationship, marriage. As a result, one must certainly agree with A. T. Robertson concerning the meaning of not being unequally yoked: "Marriage is certainly included, but other unions may be in mind."

The final three questions in this series are:

Third: "What *concord* has Christ with Bellal?"
Fourth: "What *part* does a believer have with an infidel?"
Fifth: "What *agreement* has the temple of God with idols?"

The words employed in these questions—concord, part, and agreement—serve to underscore further the futility of yoking such diverse elements together. Believers are so different in character from unbelievers that this union will not produce "concord" (from *sumphonesis,* a symphony) but disharmony. Neither do believers have any part (portion or share) in anything with unbelievers. Finally, what agreement do they have? Agreement (*sunkatathesis*) occurs only here in the New Testament. It means to approve by putting your votes together (vote for the same thing); since believers and unbelievers have different goals, they seldom see things from the same perspective.

So, the most obvious application of the prohibition of 2 Corinthians 6:14 "would be to intermarriage with the heathen" (*Expositor's Greek Testament*). The use of the related verb, *sunzeugnumi,* in Matthew 19:6 and Mark 10:9 supports this conclusion. However, as Robertson points out, it may include other relationships as well.

Any contract binding believers and unbelievers together as "partners" seems to be forbidden. Especially suspect are unequal business partnerships which are indicated by the use of the synonyms *koinonía* (fellowship) and *metoche* (partnership). Avoiding such entanglements will leave the believer free to pursue the will of God without interference from an unbelieving partner, whether in marriage or business.

10
Leave and Cleave

In answer to the question of the Pharisees concerning divorce, Jesus replied, "For this cause shall a man leave father and mother, and shall cleave to his wife: and they two shall be one flesh" (Matt. 19:5). The two key words describing a man's action in getting married are the verbs "leave" (*kataleipō*) and "cleave" (*kollaō*).

In relation to his parents, he is to "leave." This particular word for leave is formed by the combination of *leipō* (leave) and *kata* (down) and means to "leave behind." With the preposition added, *leipō* is more emphatic in meaning. In Greek literature, it often referred to leaving someone behind, especially in reference to "persons dying or going to a far country" (Liddell and Scott). Sometimes it has the even more intense meaning of "to forsake or abandon," such as the case of having to leave someone behind on the battlefield (Homer, *Iliad* 12.226).

The other pivotal word in this quotation is *kollaō* (cleave). Generally, the term means "to unite," or "join fast together." More specifically, in Greek literature it meant to glue or cement two things together (Plato, *Timaeus* 75D, 82D). In reference to metals, it meant to join one metal to another, or weld them together (Liddell and Scott).

In the New Testament, *kollaō* is used in several different contexts. It refers to: (1) the dust that sticks to one's feet as he travels through a place (Luke 10:11); (2) an illicit sexual union with a harlot (1 Cor. 6:16-17); (3) giving one's self steadfastly to that which is good (Rom. 12:9); and (4) the Prodigal attaching himself

33

to a master or patron (Luke 15:15). However, (5) *kollaō* is most often used to describe a close relationship, to keep company with a person and be on his side.

Peter uses *kollaō* when he speaks to Cornelius, "You know how that it is an unlawful thing for a man that is a Jew to *keep company,* or come unto one of another nation" (Acts 10:28; see also Acts 5:13,36; 8:29; 9:26; and 17:34).

To "leave father and mother" does not mean to abandon them totally and never return, but it does imply forsaking that relationship as one's primary earthly relationship and cleaving to one's wife. It signifies a clear-cut break with the past. To "cleave" means to be inseparably joined or welded together into one.

The marriage relationship now becomes the most vital earthly relationship. In addition, it implies that the two will now "keep company" together permanently and be on each other's side in whatever conflicts they may face.

11

Nurture and Admonition

In Ephesians 6:4, the Apostle Paul instructs fathers to bring their children up "in the nurture and admonition of the Lord." Every good parent is interested in knowing the best way of rearing his/her children. So, it is well worth our while to discover the differences between these two words which occur together in Ephesians 6:4, because they have often been "either not distinguished at all, or distinguished erroneously" (Trench).

The first word is *paideia* (nurture), which in classical Greek means "training, teaching, or education." It includes the whole instruction and training of youth, including the training of the body. While the primary idea in the word denotes mental culture or education, the word also implies the idea of correction and discipline which are sometimes necessary in achieving the primary good (Liddell and Scott). One of the more arresting uses of *paideia* was in connection with the training necessary for the practice of an art, such as music (Plato, *Symposium* 187 D). Parents are also training their children for an art, the art of Christian living. This endeavor should be worthy of all the time, discipline, and correction necessary for the pupil to excel at it.

In the later Greek of the Apocrypha and the Greek Old Testament, *paideia* assumes a somewhat modified meaning. Since the Scriptural position, based on the Old Testament, has always included loving discipline as part of the child's education (see Prov. 13:24 and 22:15), the predominant meaning of *paideia* in the Old Testament and the Apocrypha is education through discipline, instruction by correction or chastening. Examples are found in Leviticus 26:18, where punishment for sin is described, and Psalms 6:1 which states, "O Lord, rebuke me not in thine anger, neither *chasten* me in thy hot displeasure" (see also 2 Maccabees 6:12). The old Greek meaning of *paideia,* "education," is found only once in the New Testament (Acts 7:22), where it states that Moses was "educated in all the wisdom of the Egyptians."

The New Testament usage follows that of the Old Testament. The primary usage again involves chastening. *Paideia* is found three times in Hebrews 12:5-8. In each instances, it is translated "chastening" or "chastisement" and is associated with the rebuke and punishment (scourging) of the Lord. However, one should not make the mistake of concluding that *paideia* (chastening) springs from wrath. Rather it is administered in *love:* "For *whom the Lord loveth,* He chasteneth."

Paideia is employed in its verb form in Luke 23:16 and 22 with the same meaning. Pilate wanted to chasten (scourge) Jesus and let Him go. (see also Rev. 3:19; 1 Cor. 11:32; and 2 Cor. 6:9). Similarly, the early Christians' definition of the word included the idea that discipline was good for the soul; in fact, it was sometimes necessary to cleanse the heart of evil (Basil, *On Proverbs* 1).

The second word in this verse (Eph. 6:4) is *nouthesia* (admonition). It is derived from the combination of the verb *tithemi* (to place or put) and *nous* (mind); hence, it is "to put in mind" or "remind." It came to refer not only to a reminding, but also to an advising, a warning, or an admonition. Another form of the word with the letter alpha added (which has the effect of negating the word or adding the English prefix *un* to it), *anouthetetos,* refers to one who is unwarned or who refuses to be warned.

Trench describes admonition as "training by word—by the word of encouragement, when this is sufficient, but also by that of remonstrance, of reproof, of blame, where these may be required; as set over against the training by act and by discipline, which is *paideia*" (nurture). Almost everyone agrees that the distinctive feature of "admonition" is verbal instruction. Xenophon's reference to "admonishing words" clearly supports this conclusion (*Memorabilia* 1.2.21).

However, there is some disagreement over the degree of severity that admonition may include. Jerome argued in his comments on Ephesians 6:4 that "admonition" does not imply "rebuke or authority." However, Trench argues correctly that while these more severe forms of admonition are not of necessity implied, neither are they excluded. Whatever is needed to cause the admonition to be taken seriously is involved. In fact, Plato speaks of the "rod of admonition" (*Laws* 3.700C). Verbal rebuke can sometimes sting as though a person had received a whipping with a rod, and the phrase demonstrates the severity that oral rebuke may have.

Perhaps the clearest example of a strong admonition is a negative one. In the life of Eli, it is recorded that he verbally rebuked his sons for their wickedness (1 Sam. 2:24); but later it is written that he *"restrained* them not" (1 Sam. 3:13). Our word "admonish" is the same used in the Greek Old Testament for Eli's lack of severity with his sons: he did not *admonish* them.

Other passages in the New Testament where *nouthesia* is used are Titus 3:10 and 1 Corinthians 10:11, where it has the same basic meaning. The verb form of the word is found in Acts 20:31; Romans 15:14; 1 Corinthians 4:14; Colossians 1:28; 3:16; 1 Thessalonians 5:12,14; and 2 Thessalonians 3:15.

As one compares the two words, *paideia* (nurture or discipline) and *nousthesia* (admonition), it is important to see the clear line of demarcation between them. The distinction between the two is "not that between the *general* and the *special,*" but that "between training by *act and discipline* and training by *word*" (*Expositor's Greek Testament*). To raise children in a biblical, Christian manner, one must use both forms of training, or the child's education will be incomplete.

Admonition (*nousthesia*) is the milder term when it is compared to discipline (*paideia*), but even when discipline is administered, it must be accompanied with its partner, admonition (teaching and encouragement). Discipline without admonition is extremely incomplete, especially "when years advance, and there is no longer a child, but a young man, to deal with, it must give place to, or rather be swallowed up in, the *nouthesia* altogether.

And yet the *nouthesia* itself, where need is, will be earnest and severe enough" (Trench).

If the child is trained properly when he is young by the timely application of discipline and admonition (teaching, encouragement, and rebuke), the time will come, as he grows older, when the action of discipline will no longer be needed; admonition by itself will be enough.

12

Love (*Agapaō*)

The word *agapaō* (I love) in its various forms occurs over 300 times in the New Testament. However, it was never a common word in classical Greek. Since it was a little-used word for the average person, and since the pagan Greeks knew nothing of self-sacrificial love, it is used in the New Testament to "express ideas previously unknown" (W. E. Vine).

Agapaō has been described as a love which "prizes" something or someone, which "recognizes the worthiness of the object loved" (Wuest). Yet it is not an impulse based on feelings, "nor does it spend itself only upon those for whom some affinity is discovered" (Vine). It is based upon a reasoned, deliberate choice. Though it may prize someone, it is not caused by the excellency of its object (see Rom. 5:8); its cause is found in the nature and character of the one doing the loving.

When it is directed toward a person, it means "to have a preference for, wish well to, regard the welfare of" (Thayer). Examples are found in Luke 7:5 and John 11:5. When the term *agapaō* is applied to the Lord, it involves the ideas of reverence, obedience, and gratefulness for His blessings. When it is directed toward a thing, it means "to take pleasure in the thing, prize it above other things, be unwilling to abandon it, or do without it" (Thayer; see Heb. 1:9 and 2 Tim. 4:10).

In the New Testament, *Agapaō* describes the attitude of God toward His Son (John 17:26), the human race (John 3:16), and believers (John 14:21). It denotes God's will for His children in their attitude toward one another (John 13:34). Finally, it expresses the essential nature of God; "God is *Agape*" (1 John 4:8—noun form used).

This kind of love can be seen only through the actions of those who have it. God has expressed His love perfectly in sending Jesus; persons demonstrate their love to God through their obedience to Him. This kind of love involves two things: (1) selflessness (putting another's welfare above one's own) and (2) commitment (a reasoned choice to love someone regardless of the cost or the situation).

13

Love (*Phileō*)

The word *phileo* (I love) denotes a type of love which is characterized by a certain "fondness, liking, or affection for" a person or thing. It is a more instinctive kind of love than is *agapao* and is usually the result of natural affections (Trench). In other words, it is the kind of love a person is likely to have for someone with whom he has something in common, or for someone who has qualities "which are agreeable to us" (Wuest).

While *phileō* is not always an unreasoning kind of affection, it does seem to be prompted by the senses and emotions rather than reason. For this reason in the New Testament we are never commanded to *phileō*. And, because love as an emotion cannot be commanded, only love which is given through a deliberate choice may be commanded (*agapaō*). Neither are husbands told to *phileō* their wives because it is assumed that they would already have a fondness for them and an emotional attachment to them.

The contrast between *phileō* and *agapaō* is seen vividly in John 21:15-17, where Jesus asked Peter twice if he loved Him (had an unselfish commitment *to*—*agapaō*) and Peter answered twice that he loved Him (had a fondness based on common goals—*phileō*). Peter never claimed to have a superior love but protested that he loved Jesus like a friend. The third time Jesus used the word *phileō*. By this Jesus meant, even if Peter had only this kind of love, he should feed the Lord's sheep (John 21:17).

41

14

Wisdom

In his letter to the Colossians, the apostle Paul prays for the brethren that they will have "wisdom and understanding" in the knowledge of God's will (Col. 1:9). The word for wisdom is *sophia*. The central idea of this concept of wisdom is "insight into the true nature of things."

In secular Greek literature, *sophia* referred to several different things. First, it denoted skill or cleverness in any one of a variety of things, such as, art, carpentry, music, driving, or medicine. Next, it described skill in matters of common, everyday life; it spoke of sound judgment or practical wisdom. Finally, it referred to knowledge of a higher kind, such as learning in science or philosophy (see Liddell and Scott).

Sophia is variously used in the Scriptures. (1) It most properly describes God (Rom. 11:33). (2) The people of Jesus' day recognized that He had wisdom and were astonished—perhaps because they expected that only God should have such wisdom, and some of them did not understand that He was God (Matt. 13:54). (3) On a few occasions, wisdom is personified by the writers of the New Testament (Matt. 11:19; Luke 11:49). In this sense, it usually refers to the Old Testament or a truth Jesus spoke. (4) It is often used to describe human wisdom; however, a distinction is almost always made between true wisdom which comes only from God (1 Cor. 12:8; Acts 6:10) and man's natural wisdom.

In fact, Trench makes the observation that *sophia* is "never in Scripture ascribed to other than God or good men, except in an

ironical sense," and with the express addition "of this world" (1
Cor. 1:20), "of this age" (1 Cor. 2:6), or some other similar designa-
tion. He further adds that neither are "the children of this world
called *sophoi* except with this tacit or expressed irony (Luke 10:-
21)."

In conclusion, a person can only be called wise when he is
acquainted with divine matters and has profound insight into the
principles by which God operates in this world.

15

Understanding

A sister concept to wisdom (*sophia*) is understanding. While understanding is similar to wisdom, it definitely has a distinct meaning of its own. On two occasions, Paul links the two concepts, and in both passages these concepts are connected with the idea of knowing God's will. However, he uses two different Greek words for understanding. In Ephesians 1:8, he speaks of God's "wisdom and understanding" (*phronesis*) in making known to us "the mystery of His will." In Colossians 1:9, Paul desires that believers might have "wisdom and understanding" (*sunesis*) of God's will.

The first word, *phronesis,* was used by the ancient philosophers relative to a right application of the mind. It means to have "insight into or understanding of" something. But more than that, it refers to a manner of thinking. It means to form an opinion based on sober thinking. As Trench writes, *phronesis* "has a practical character to it"—it acts. The verb form of the word (*phroneo*) involves concentration of the mind on something in order to achieve a good end. In contrast, *sunesis* describes the critical facility of the mind, referring to reflective thought which seeks to analyze another person or thing.

When we put the three words together, a clear distinction is evident. First, the believer is to have wisdom (*sophia*), which is the ability to understand the basic or elementary principles about God and the way He operates (see 1 Cor. 12:8). Next, the ability is needed to reflect upon these principles (*sunesis*) and apply them "to any given situation" which may arise in life (Barclay).[3] Finally, a practical insight is needed to transfer these academic conclusions concerning life into action (*phronesis*).

16
Submission

One of the most controversial pronouncements by the apostle Paul is found in Colossians 3:18, where he writes, "Wives, submit yourselves unto your own husbands, as it is fit in the Lord." The same admonition is given in Ephesians 5:22 also, although in this case the verb is understood from the preceding verse. The key word in this command is "submit" (*hupotassō*), which is a compound word made up of *hupo* (under) and *tassō* (to arrange).

In classical Greek, *hupotassō* had its primary usage as a military term, "to rank under." In addition, it meant to subject or subdue, as Pompey did those whom he conquered (Plutarch, *Pompey* 64). In logic, it meant "to take as a minor premise." A similar meaning for *hupotassō* is "to follow" (Liddell and Scott).

In the New Testament, this word has a variety of applications. First, it is used in the active voice primarily of God. It means to bring someone or something into subjection. Paul says, "He has put all things in subjection under His feet" (Heb. 2:8; see also 1 Cor. 15:27-28). He has the power to "subdue all things to Himself" (Phil. 3:21 and Romans 8:20).

In most cases, however, *hupotassō* is directed to human beings in the middle voice which means "to submit or yield to another's authority." (1) The most frequent application of the word is in reference to wives and husbands. In addition to the two passages already mentioned, it is used in Titus 2:5 (*"submissive* to their own husbands"); 1 Peter 3:1,5 ("wives, be in subjection to your own husbands"); and 1 Corinthians 14:34 ("for it is not permitted unto them to speak, but to be submissive"). (2) A different use of the word is found in Luke 2:51. Jesus "was subject" to His parents. This use clearly illustrates the fact that *hupotasso* does not imply that the one being submissive is inferior to the authority placed over him in any way. But then, neither does superiority give one an excuse for not being submissive to authority. For even though Jesus was superior to His parents in every respect, He still accepted their authority over Him as part of the will of the Father for Him.

Other uses of submission include: (3) slaves to masters (Titus 2:9; 1 Peter 2:18); (4) believers to the secular authorities (Romans 13:1,5; Titus 3:1; 1 Peter 2:13); (5) members to church officials (1 Peter 5:5; 1 Cor. 16:16); (6) believers to God (1 Cor. 15:28; Heb. 12:9; James 4:7); (7) believers to Christ (Eph. 5:24); (8) unbelievers not submissive to the will of God (Rom. 8:7; 10:3); and (9) believers to one another in the Lord (Eph. 5:21).

There are two final references which do not fit any of the above categories. The spirits of the prophets were "subject to the prophets" (1 Cor. 14:32), and the demons were subject to the seventy who went out in the name of Jesus (Luke 10:17,20).

In conclusion: (1) the verb *hupotasso* is used in a great variety of contexts in the New Testament, and in every one of them the same basic meaning applies—"to arrange or place under" someone or something. (2) Only God appears as one who has power and authority to subdue anyone under His authority. No person is told to force anyone else to be subject to him. In every case the command is to the one who is to be submissive, such as "Wives, submit *yourselves,*" not "Husbands, subdue your wives." (3) Finally, there is no hint of inferiority in the word *hupotasso,* but only the challenge of accepting God's "arrangement" for a given relationship in your life.

17
Called Christians

In Acts 11:26 it is recorded that the disciples were first "called Christians" at Antioch. Both of these words are interesting, especially since they are used together. The first word, "called" (*chrematizō*), is interesting because it is not the common word for "call" in the New Testament (*kaleō*). The primary meaning for this word is to transact business; a second meaning is related to the first. It refers to the giving of advice to those who enquired concerning official statements by the magistrates, or it may refer to those consulting the oracle of a god (Josephus, *Antiquities* 5.1.14).

In the Scriptures, it is used both in the Old and New Testaments in reference to those who have been warned of God about something in particular (Acts 10:22; Jer. 33:2, 37:2). Finally, *chrematizō* means to assume a name for oneself from one's public business—to receive a title. It is used twice in the New Testament in this sense. Besides the passage already mentioned, it occurs in Romans 7:3: "She shall be called an adultress." This woman received a bad name as a result of the way she conducted her business.

At Antioch, the Christians received their name in three ways. First, they received it because of the way they conducted their business; they were called Christians because this *was* their chief business. Second, they received the name because they were constantly answering questions people had and giving out the message of God. Third, they received that name because it was in His name

48

that they received the power to change their lives. The title they received, Christians, means belonging to Christ (Messiah).

It is not clear from the word itself whether the believers gave themselves the name or were given the name by others; however, the context leads us to believe that this was a "name given to the followers of Christ by Gentiles to distinguish them from Jews" (A. T. Robertson). The Jews would not call them Christians (belonging to Messiah) because they did not accept Jesus as Messiah. By the Jews, they were called Galileans or Nazarenes. The followers of Christ called themselves "disciples," "believing brethren," "saints," or "those of the way."

It is understandable, then, that the three uses of *chrematizo* in the New Testament all come from the heathen viewpoint: (1) Agrippa uses it as a term of contempt (Acts 26:28); (2) Peter employs it in connection with persecution by the Roman government (1 Pet. 4:16); and (3) the pagans at Antioch utilize it to refer to the believers (Acts 11:26).

This conclusion is also in accordance with other pagan writings. The Roman writer Tacitus called Christians "a class of people loathed for their vices, who were commonly styled Christian after Christ, who was executed by the procurator Pontius Pilate when Tiberius was emperor" (*Annals* 15. 44). Suetonius added, "Punishment was inflicted on the Christians, a class of men addicted to a mischievous and novel superstition" (*Life of Nero* 16. 2).

Although these writers meant their comments to be derogatory in nature, they could hardly have paid the disciples any greater compliment than to call them Christians. Such proved that their lives had conveyed the exact message they had wanted to present— that they belonged to Jesus the Messiah.

18

Confess

In 1 John 1:9, the Bible declares, "If we confess our sins, He is faithful and just to forgive us our sins and cleanse us from all unrighteousness." The word for confess is *homologeō*, which means literally "to say the same thing." Although this phrase is the central idea conveyed by *homologeō*, there are five different senses in which it is used.

(1) It means to agree with someone or something (concede). In the Greek papyri of the New Testament period, it is used to refer to the making of a contract in general, and especially of persons at war agreeing to the terms of surrender (Wuest; see Heb. 11:13).

(2) The most frequent use of *homologeō* is to refer to the confession of guilt either to God, as in the passage mentioned above, or to men. Paul admits that he is guilty of being a Christian in Acts 24:14.

(3) In a more positive way, this term is used to denote the act of openly declaring oneself to be a follower of Christ (profess Christ): "If you confess with the mouth the Lord Jesus . . ." (Rom. 10:9; see also Matt. 10:32).

(4) Another implication of the word *homologeō* is clearly seen in Matthew 14:7, where Herod "confessed" to Herodias's daughter, Salome. This use of the word involves the making of a promise.

(5) Finally, the most unusual use of the word is found in Hebrews 13:15: "Therefore by Him let us continually offer the sacrifice of praise to God, that is, the fruit of our lips giving thanks (*homologounton*) to His name." Confession of Christ is a celebra-

tion of praise to God. When a person confesses his sin to God, in essence he is doing all of the above-mentioned things. He is agreeing to God's terms of surrender; he is admitting his guilt; he is confessing that he is now going to be a follower of Christ; he is sealing a promise to follow Jesus as his Lord; and he is making a sacrifice of praise to God.

19

God Is Willing

One of the most controversial texts in today's theological discussions is 2 Peter 3:9, which says, "God is not willing that any should perish but that all should come to repentance." The discussion centers around the word "willing" (*boulomai*) and whether or not God really desires all men to repent.

In classical Greek *boulomai* means "to will, wish, or be willing." At times it is used to mean a mere wish or inclination as compared to the verb *thelō,* which expresses will in the sense of choice or purpose (Liddell and Scott), but this distinction cannot always be maintained. Some interpreters, however, insist on translating *boulomai* in 2 Peter 3:9: "not *wishing* that any should perish." But it should be noted that the poet Homer always uses *boulomai* instead of *thelō* when referring to the gods, because with them wish is will (Liddell and Scott).

By the first century there was no longer a difference between *thelō* and *boulomai.* Both Plato and Josephus use the words interchangeably (Arndt). Both also use the noun form *boulema* to express God's will.

In the New Testament, *boulomai* denotes: (1) to want or desire something, such as "a desire to be rich" (1 Tim. 6:9), and (2) decisions of the will after some deliberation, as in James 1:18—"Of his own will begat he us with the word of truth" (see also Matt. 11:27 and 1 Cor. 12:11). W. E. Vine concluded that *boulomai* usually expresses the deliberate exercise of volition more strongly than *thelō.* Whether or not this conclusion is correct, is not certain;

however, this question is academic, since *thelō* is also used to express God's will for "all men to be saved" (1 Tim. 2:4).

If God has an intense desire for all men to be saved (the noun form *boulema* means design, intent, or purpose), why then are they *not* all saved?

It is evident that God has the power to bring about His will (*boulema*), but He has chosen not to do it by force. The only explanation is that each man has been allowed the choice of receiving or rejecting God's offer of salvation in Christ. Moreover, since God wants all men to be saved, the church must also want all men to be saved, whether they be rich or poor, good or bad.

20

The Deacon

A *diakonos* (deacon) is one who executes the commands of another, a servant. He is, however, a servant in the nature of his work, one who serves others, not in his relation to a person who is his master. He is not a slave, as the word *doulos* denotes, but he is a servant voluntarily (Trench).

The word *diakonos* is used in reference to the servants of a king, such as in Matthew 22:1ff. In this passage the king addresses two different kinds of servants: those who delivered the invitations were *douloi* (22:3), and those who cast out the improperly dressed guest were *diakonoi* (22:13).

Another common deployment of the word is to denote a waiter, one who serves food and drink. This use of the word is found in the writings of Xenophon (*Memorabilia* 1.5.2), and a similar usage is seen in Herodotus (*The History* 4.71). It is used in three New Testament passages with this emphasis. The servants who drew the water and served the wine at the marriage feast in Cana are called *diakonoi* (John 2:5,9). The servants in Jesus' parable of the marriage feast who were commanded to bind the man without a wedding garment were "deacons." Finally, the verb form of the word is used of Martha who *served* a meal for Jesus (John 12:2).

Another interesting use of the word in its verb form in the Greek papyri is to refer to the serving of an apprenticeship by a young boy to a weaver (Milligan). In the New Testament, *diakonos* also refers to a servant of the gospel (Col. 1:23), a minister of Jesus

Christ (1 Tim. 4:6), and a minister of the church (Col. 1:25). The most well-known translation of the word, however, is "deacon," an officer of the church. Originally, the deacon was one who waited on tables (Acts 6), but his ministry is not limited to that one duty; he is a servant of the Lord and the church.

21

The Bishop

The *episcopos* (bishop or overseer) in the Greek Old Testament is almost always an official who was in charge of work being done, such as repairs on the Temple (2 Kings 11:18) or the rebuilding of Jerusalem (Neh. 11:9). Occasionally it refers to an officer in the army (Judges 9:28).

Among the Greeks, *episcopos* was an official title. It could signify a commissioner appointed to regulate a new colony or an inspector who reported to the king. Antiochus Epiphanes, in an attempt to stop the worship of Jehovah God, appointed commissioners (overseers) to see that his orders were obeyed (1 Maccabees 1:51). The fundamental idea of the word is inspection, and "its usage suggests two subsidiary notions also: (1) Responsibility to a superior power; (2) The introduction of a new order of things" (J. B. Lightfoot).

In the New Testament "it is almost universally admitted to be synonymous with *presbuteros*" or elder (H. A. A. Kennedy). Examples of the interchanging of these terms is found in Titus 1:5-7; 1 Timothy 3:2-5 and 5:17-19; and Acts 20:17,28. In the final passage mentioned, Acts 20:28, Luke addresses the elders of the church at Ephesus and calls them "overseers" (bishops) of the flock. In addition, he tells these "elderbishops" that they are to "pastor" the church of God, thus indicating that the terms pastor, elder, and bishop all signify the same office.

In conclusion, the *episcopos* is a man charged with the duty of seeing that things to be done by others are done correctly. Spiritually, he is a guardian of souls—one who watches over their welfare (1 Pet. 2:25).

22

Judge Not

One of the best-known sayings of Jesus is found in Matthew 7:1, which states, "Judge not that ye be not judged." Just what did Jesus mean when he said, "Judge not"? The word used here is the verb *krinō*, which originally meant "to separate, select, or choose." In Greek literature it is used in a variety of ways. It could mean "to estimate, interpret, or decide (judge) a matter." The Athenian poets used it with the meaning to (1) accuse, (2) question, or (3) condemn someone or something (Liddell and Scott).

In the New Testament it is applied to: (1) God who "shall judge the quick and the dead" (2 Tim. 4:1); (2) the word of God that shall judge those who reject the Lord (John 12:48); (3) men who are appointed by God to judge such as the apostles (Matt. 19:28; in the Old Testament it is used concerning the rule of kings—2 Kings 15:5); and (4) the saints who someday will judge both the world and the angels (1 Cor. 6:2).

Several uses of the word *krinō* (judge) are directed toward believers in particular. These uses can be divided into two categories: those things which are forbidden and those which are allowed or encouraged. On one hand, believers are commanded *not* to: (1) criticize or find fault in others (Rom. 14:3,10,13*a* and Col. 2:16); (2) assume the role of a judge and condemn someone ("Judge not that ye be not judged," Matt. 7:1; see also John 8:15); and (3) take other believers to court before unbelieving judges (1 Cor. 6:6).

On the other hand, believers are instructed to discern (consider) the difference between right and wrong. Paul says, "Judge in

58

yourselves; it is comely that a woman pray unto God uncovered" (1 Cor. 11:13; see also Rom. 14:5; Acts 15:19; and Luke 7:43). After a situation has been considered, one should reach a decision (resolve or determine) about his course of action. Paul says to the Corinthians, "But I determined (judged) this with myself, that I would not come again to you in heaviness" (2 Cor. 2:1; see also 1 Cor. 7:37). Finally, believers collectively are to discipline (judge) any believer living in open sin for the offender's own good (1 Cor. 5:3,12).

In conclusion, judging for the purpose of condemning or criticizing another is prohibited in the New Testament. However, judging in the sense of discerning another's spiritual condition for the purpose of helping him is not only permitted but commanded.

23

Church

The word *ekklesía* (church) refers to the lawful assembly in a free Greek city state of those who possessed citizenship and were summoned by the town crier. In Athens, for example, the ordinary assembly met four times during each legislative period (presidency) of thirty-five or thirty-six days. The word is a compound of *ek* and *klesis* and literally means "the called-out ones." It therefore does not refer to the entire population of any place, but a select portion of it (Trench). Only once, however, does the New Testament use this word with its earlier Greek political significance. In Acts 19:32,39, and 41, it refers to an assembly of citizens at Ephesus.

In the Septuagint it is often used to denote the assembly of the Israelites (Judges 21:9; Joshua 8:35). The New Testament also employs the word once in this sense referring to the Jewish assembly in the wilderness (Acts 7:38). However, the idea of people who are "called out" is not as clearly evident in the Old Testament usage.

Only in New Testament times did the word *ekklesía* reach its highest glory. It has come to denote three concepts in its Christian usage. *Ekklesía* refers to:

(1) an assembly of Christians gathered together for worship (1 Cor. 11:18; 14:19,35),

(2) the totality of Christians living in one place, such as in any city (Acts 5:11; 8:1), or even in one house (Rom. 16:5), and

(3) the assembly to which all believers belong (Eph. 1:22, 3:10,21; Col. 1:18,24).

The tracing of this word's history is another great example of the "progressive ennobling" of a word which ascended from an ordinary usage to a holy one.

24

Repent

The primary word in the New Testament for repent is *meta-noeō*. It means in classical Greek to change one's mind (opinion) or purpose after some reflection on the past. In secular usage, the change may be for the good or for the bad.

Trench lists several instances of repentance from good to evil. One of these occurs in Plutarch who cited an instance where two murderers decided to spare the life of a child, but after reflection changed their minds on the matter. In its New Testament usage it is limited to religious or ethical matters. As Thayer says, *metanoeō* is "used especially of those who, conscious of their sins and with manifest tokens of sorrow, are intent upon obtaining God's pardon."

Wuest also agrees that the ideas of sorrow and contrition with respect to sin are included in the biblical use of the word. Trench lists four ideas that are included in the meaning of *metanoeō:* (1) it means to know (perceive) afterwards as opposed to *pronoeō* (to know beforehand); (2) it signifies the change of mind which comes as a result of this knowledge; (3) it involves regret for the course pursued (displeasure at one's own self); and (4) it signifies a change of conduct for the future based on this change of mind.

The idea of sorrow and the idea of a change of behavior are both closely connected with the concept of repentance. However, strictly speaking, sorrow is not to be equated with repentance (*metanoeō*). As Paul says, "For godly sorrow worketh repentance (*metanoeō*) to salvation not to be repented of (*ametameleton*): but the sorrow of the world worketh death" (2 Cor. 7:10). While it may be impossible to repent without feeling some measure of sorrow for sin, it is quite possible to feel sorrow for sin without repenting of sin at all.

Part of the confusion over this point is in the fact that another word (*metamelomai*) is also translated to mean repent five times in the New Testament. While it is sometimes used with the same force as *metanoeō*, its basic meaning is "to have an after-care" or "a second thought over a matter." Judas is an example of this type of repentance (Matt. 27:3). He was troubled in mind over his sin and wished he had not done it, but went no further. Forgiveness is never promised for this kind of attitude. (See the use of this word also in Hebrews 7:21 where the Lord swore and will not repent, and the verse already cited, 2 Cor. 7:10, where the one having true repentance will not need to have second thoughts over his decision.)

Concerning the idea of a change in behavior, it must be understood that the change itself is not repentance but the *result* of repentance. John the Baptist preached repentance (Matt. 3:2), and then he demanded that the people bring forth "fruits worthy of repentance" (Matt. 3:8). Repentance (*metanoeō*) expresses mental direction from evil and toward God and good works (Acts 8:22, 26:20); it represents a change in one's purpose.

But then, how can one see a change in our minds except through a change in the way we conduct ourselves? In addition, since repentance is basically a mental decision at first, a mere emotional appeal to a sinner will not suffice—one must convince him in his mind of the truth of the Scriptures.

25

Acts 2:38 and Baptismal Regeneration

For centuries there has been considerable controversy concerning the meaning of Acts 2:38, which reads, "Then Peter said unto them, Repent, and be baptized every one of you in the name of Jesus Christ *for* the remission of sins, and ye shall receive the gift of the Holy Ghost." Some argue on the basis of this one verse that a person *must be baptized* in order to be saved.

It is further contended that others are denying the Scripture when they translate this verse, "Repent and be baptized *because of* the remission of sins." To answer this question, one must first consider the meaning of the Greek word *eis* (for) in Acts 2:38. One group declares that *eis* can only be used as "prospective, looking to an end to be reached, purpose, or aim." It is further stated that no recognized Greek-English lexicon gives the word *eis* the meaning "because of." While the following is by no means a complete list, it is enough to show that this contention is incorrect.

John Pickering (at one time president of the American Academy of Arts and Sciences), in his work *A Comprehensive Lexicon of the Greek New Testament,* lists the following meanings for *eis:* into, on, to, towards, against, upon, because of, with respect to, upon account of, among, through, and for.

Liddell and Scott's *Greek-English Lexicon* also lists "in regard to" and "in relation to" as possible meanings. This would mean that the remission of sins is related to baptism, but not necessarily the purpose of baptism.

The New International Dictionary of New Testament Theology, which is edited by Colin Brown, discusses the use of prepositions at length and says concerning *eis:*

> Since elsewhere John's baptism is termed a "baptism of (-relating to, marked by) repentance," "a repentance baptism" (Mk. 1:14; Lk. 3:3; Acts 13:24; 19:4), *eis* may simply mean "in relation or reference to." Similarly, in Acts 2:38 forgiveness of sin could be the purpose of repentance and baptism (final or telic *eis*) (cf. I Pet. 3:21) or their outcome (ecbatic or consecutive *eis*), or else forgiveness is being regarded as conceptually (but not necessarily chronologically) coincident with baptism (*eis*-temporal *en*) or as connected with baptism (referential *eis*).

Arndt and Gingrich's *A Greek-English Lexicon of the New Testament* also lists the causal use of *eis* (because of) as one of the lesser used, but nevertheless legitimate, meanings of the word.

Furthermore, there are many works on Greek syntax which discuss the causal use of *eis* (because of). For exampls, see Dana and Mantey, *A Manual Grammer of the New Testament,* pp. 103-105; Brooks and Winberry, *Syntax of New Testament Greek,* p. 56; or Robertson and Davis, *A New Short Grammar of the Greek Testament,* pp. 255-256.

In addition to these works on the Greek language, there is other evidence which cannot be ignored: the casual use of *eis* is found in the New Testament itself. Luke 11:32 says, "For they repented at (*eis* with the sense of "because of") the preaching of Jonah." Romans 4:20 says, "He staggered not at the promise of God through (*eis*) the preaching of Jonah." Evidently, the translators of the King James Version were aware of this usage.

The second problem in Acts 2:38 is the relationship of the two verbs "repent and be baptized." Some argue that they must be taken together as two things necessary for salvation. However, it is clear that there is a break in the thought between the two verbs in the Greek text which is not preserved in the English translation. The first verb (repent) is in the second person plural: "repent ye", but the second one (be baptized) is in the third person singular: "let each one be baptized." Why is there a change unless the two thoughts are to be separated? "Repent" is in the plural because it is directed to the whole crowd present that day. "Be baptized" is singular because it is addressed to each one who has repented.

The fundamental question, however, is not whether Acts 2:38 can be understood as agreeing with the position of salvation by faith alone, but whether the contention that baptism is necessary for salvation can be reconciled with the rest of the New Testament. Just a few of the problems with this view will be cited.

(1) The thief on the cross next to Jesus was saved without baptism (Luke 23:43). (2) The Gentiles were told in Acts 10:43, "Whosoever believeth in him shall receive remission of sins." While they were listening to the preaching of Peter, the Gentiles believed in Christ, received the Spirit, and spoke in tongues (Acts 10:46). All of this occurred *before* Peter asked if anyone would deny their right to be baptized. Who can deny that receiving the Holy Spirit is proof of one's salvation?

(3) Paul clearly states in 1 Corinthians 1:17 that baptism is not part of the gospel when he says: "For Christ sent me not to baptize, but to preach the gospel." Baptism is clearly not a part of the gospel, according to Paul. He adds, "I thank God that I baptized none of you, but Crispus and Gaius" (1 Cor. 1:14). These statements are totally incompatible with the idea of baptismal regeneration.

(4) If this were not enough, Paul's two great works on the doctrine of salvation, Romans and Galatians, give the most detailed discussions of salvation found in the Bible. Both conclude that a man is justified by faith without the deeds of the law (Rom. 3:22-24,28, 5:1; Gal. 2:16). In fact, the entire fourth chapter of Romans was written to show that Abraham was declared righteous by faith before he was circumcised (Rom. 4:9-11). Circumcision was the sign of obedience to the old covenant just as baptism is a sign of obedience to the new covenant. If the analogy is followed, it is clear that baptism is not a part of salvation, but a sign that one has salvation.

Since baptism is a work which one can perform, salvation by faith plus baptism amounts to salvation by works, and this is in direct contradiction to the grace of God. Paul says, "Therefore, it is of faith that it might be according to grace" (Rom. 4:16), and "Whosoever of you are justified by the law; ye are fallen from grace" (Gal. 5:4).

The conclusion of the whole matter is: it is a dangerous matter to base one's entire interpretation of the Bible on one word which has numerous meanings. Difficult passages should be interpreted in the light of the whole Bible. If this principle is followed, one will not come up with interpretations which contradict the whole spirit and content of the Scriptures.

26
Meekness

The Greek word *praotes* is one for which there is no exact English equivalent. It has generally been translated by the word "meekness." However, there are connotations of weakness implied in that word which are not accurate at all. Yet, it is still used for lack of a better word.

The ancients also had trouble defining this word and, like us, usually ended up describing more of what it is not than what it is. Aristotle described it as that happy medium between too much and too little anger (*Rhetoric 2.3.1*). Plutarch in *Concerning Lack of Gall* contrasted *praotes* with severity, and Plato (*Symposiacs* 197 D) described it as the opposite of fierceness or cruelty—that is, mildness or gentleness.

About this word Trench writes, "The Scriptural *praotes* is not in a man's outward behaviour only; nor yet in his relations to his fellow-men; . . . Rather it is an inwrought grace of the soul; and the exercises of it are first and chiefly towards God (Matt. 11:29; James 1:21). It is that temper of spirit in which we accept his dealings with us as good, and therefore without disputing or resisting." He further indicates that meekness is closely connected with humility for only a humble heart can possibly be meek. Barclay describes the meek man as one who is "so self-controlled, because he is God-controlled, that he is always angry at the right time and never angry at the wrong time" (Barclay on Col. 3:12).[4]

Perhaps the best illustration of what *praotes* means is found in classical Greek where it is used to describe a horse who is gentle and tame (Liddell and Scott). He is powerful but gentle. When applied to a person it means two things. First, it means that one has the inner strength to maintain self-control, even in the face of insult or injury. He does not lash out at his enemies because he can restrain himself through the power of God (Gal. 5:23), but he is not afraid to oppose evil when it is necessary to do so (2 Tim. 2:25; Gal. 6:1). Second, in relation to God, it refers to a person who is submissive and teachable, willing to learn to do things God's way. He is not consumed with self-interest and does not put himself forward, but is willing to defer to a higher authority (Josh. 1:21).

The ultimate example of meekness is Jesus. Matthew 11:29 says of Him, "I am meek and lowly in heart." All of the qualities mentioned above are true of Him, and no one could ever charge that there was any weakness in Him, for He had all the power of God at His disposal!

27
Joy

The principal word for joy in the New Testament is *chara*. In classical Greek it was used to describe "joy in or at a thing," such as the "joy" of a hungry person at the sight of food. In the New Testament it is translated "joy" and sometimes "gladness." It is the opposite of *lupe* (sorrow).

Paul's epistle to the Philippians is called the "epistle of joy" because it describes in detail those virtues in which the believer finds joy. First, there is the joy which one experiences because of his relationship to the body of Christ. (1) There is the joy of Christian fellowship with those with the same love and mind (Phil. 2:2). (2) There is joy in receiving good news from a loved one (2:28). (3) The person who provides hospitality will experience joy in so doing (2:29). As William Barclay writes, "It is a great thing to have a door from which the stranger and the one in trouble know that they will never be turned away."[5] (4) Next, there is the joy that comes from a man who has won others to the Lord and has had the privilege of seeing them grow in the Lord. Paul told the Philippians that they were his "joy and crown" (4:1). (5) Finally, Paul experienced the joy of receiving a gift from those who cared for him (4:10).

In addition to that mentioned above, there is the joy, also mentioned in Philippians, which comes as a result of our fellowship with the Lord. (1) There is the gladness one experiences through prayer (1:4). (2) The true disciple of the Lord will experience joy whenever the good news about Jesus is preached (1:18). (3) There is the joy of faith in Christ (1:25). Again Barclay comments, "If Christianity does not make a man happy, it will not make him anything at all."[6]

(4) Paul also mentions the joy he has because of the opportunity given him to suffer for Christ. There are many other examples of this type of joy in the Scriptures. The cross was a "joy" set before Jesus (Heb. 12:2). The early church rejoiced that they were counted worthy of suffering for His name (Acts 5:41). (5) Finally, there is the joy of being in Christ (Phil. 3:1, 4:4). He is the only source of true joy. The fruit of His Spirit is love, *joy,* and peace (Gal. 5:22). Those who live according to His will, whatever it brings, will be rewarded with "the joy of the Lord" (Matt. 25:21,23).

28

Infallible Proofs

In Acts 1:3, the Bible says that Jesus "presented Himself alive after His suffering by many *infallible proofs*" which took place during the forty days between the resurrection and the ascension. The word translated "infallible proofs" in the King James Version is *tekmerion,* a word which is used nowhere else in the New Testament. It refers to that which is a sure or positive sign, a convincing or decisive proof. In the work of Aristotle it refers to a proof which can be demonstrated, one which is the opposite to the fallible sign, *semeion.* The philosopher writes, "Of these, the second, the conclusive sign, is called *tekmerion* . . . , for when people take what they have said to be irrefutable, they think they proffer a *tekmerion,* as if the matter were now demonstrated and concluded" (*Rhetoric* 1.2.17). The verb form of the word is used in inter-Biblical literature with the meaning to show or prove by sure signs "that from which something is surely and plainly known" (3 Maccabees 3:24).

Some modern translations of the Bible drop the word "infallible" and simply translate the word "proofs." This action follows the reasoning given by W. E. Vine who says, "A proof does not require to be described as infallible." While technically this is true, it is also desirable that believers know that the post-resurrection appearances are not simply fallible evidences pointing to the truth of Jesus' claims, but incontrovertible proof that Jesus is, in fact, alive.

29

Hope

In classical Greek literature the word *elpis* (hope) refers to anxious thoughts concerning the future, a fear or expectation depending on whether the thing hoped for would be good or bad. In the New Testament, however, the word is always used in reference to something good. The "hope" of the Christian is a "joyful and confident expectation of eternal salvation" (Thayer), which is in direct contrast to the person without God who has no hope (Eph. 2:12).

W. E. Vine summarizes the New Testament usage of the word into three categories: (1) Hope is the happy anticipation of good. There is the hope of the righteousness which is by faith (Gal. 5:5), the hope of salvation (1 Thess. 5:8), the hope of eternal life (Tit. 1:2, 3:7), the hope of the glory of God (Rom. 5:2), and the blessed hope and glorious appearing of the Savior (Tit. 2:13). All of this sums up what Paul calls the "hope of Israel" (Acts 28:20).

(2) In addition, there is the ground upon which hope in the New Testament is based. The basis for the believer's hope is the resurrection of Christ. Paul says that we have a "hope, even the resurrection" (Acts 23:6). Further, the hope of the Christian is based on the promise of God (Acts 26:6-7) which is found in the gospel (Col. 1:23). In Acts 26:6 Paul says, "And now I stand and am judged for the hope of the promise made of God unto our fathers." Moreover, if one receives the promises of God in Christ, he may know the confident assurance (hope) of His calling (Eph. 1:18).

Finally, the source of this hope lies in God himself. In Romans 15:13, God is described as the "God of hope," the one who causes believers to "abound in hope." (3) The object upon which the Christian's hope is fixed is the Lord Jesus Christ (1 Tim. 1:1). When a person fixes his hope in Christ there will be several results: his life will be purified (1 John 3:3); he will gain endurance so his soul will have an anchor against the storms of life (1 Thess. 1:3; Heb. 6:18-19); and the one with this hope will have the full assurance of his salvation which is in Christ (Heb. 6:11).

30

New Testament Wine

Many Christians through the years have debated the issue of whether the wine mentioned in the New Testament was fermented or unfermented, and the question is still being asked today. A look at the words for wine in the New Testament will shed a certain amount of light on this question.

While the Greeks had several words for wine and other similar beverages, only two words for wine are used in the New Testament. The first word is *gleukos,* which refers to a sweet, new wine. The only New Testament use of *gleukos* is in Acts 2:13, when the disciples are accused of drinking too much of it. The accusation shows that it must have undergone some fermentation and become an intoxicant.

The primary word for wine, which is used in all of the other references to wine in the New Testament, is *oinos.* Originally, the word applied to the fermented juice of the grape (Liddell and Scott). In the Septuagint it is used to translate the Hebrew word *tirosh,* which refers to the fruit of the vine in its natural condition (Hos. 4:11), as well as *yayin* (fermented or unfermented grape juice). By New Testament times the word has a more general usage and may refer to different types of wine (both the fermented and unfermented).

Some would argue that *oinos* always refers to fermented wine in the New Testament, because there is another word for unfermented juice or "must" (*trux*) which is available, but it is never used. In addition, it is charged that since the grape juice would

75

naturally ferment, it could not be kept long without fermentation. The first of these contentions is inconclusive by itself, and the second is incorrect.

The ancients had four methods of preserving unfermented juice. They could: (1) boil it and keep it as a thick syrup, (2) filter it through sand or other materials to remove yeast, (3) let the yeast settle to the bottom, pour off the pure juice, and keep it in a cool place, or (4) introduce substances that would inhibit the action of the yeast. In New Testament times, however, the normal usage of the word is for the fermented juice of the grape (Arndt), but one must examine the context of each reference to be certain which type of drink is denoted.

In the New Testament itself, most of the uses of *oinos* appear to refer to fermented wine. The bursting of the old wineskins by new wine implies fermentation (Matt. 9:17; Mark 2:22; Luke 5:37). The command to "Be not drunk with wine" (Eph. 5:18) clearly refers to fermented wine, and the warnings against addiction to wine and excess of wine no doubt do also (I Tim. 3:3, 8; Tit. 1:7, 2:3; and 1 Peter 4:3). In Romans 14:21, drinking wine was described by some Christians as an "occasion of stumbling," so it must be generally understood to refer to an intoxicant. Even the most disputed passage, Jesus' turning the water to wine (John 2:3ff.), appears to denote fermented wine because of the comment that old wine was considered to be superior to new wine (Luke 5:39).

Another use of *oinos,* besides the use of wine as a beverage, is the medicinal use. It was used internally to settle the stomach and aid digestion (I Tim. 5:23), and externally, to sterilize wounds. The Good Samaritan poured oil and wine on the injured man's wounds (Luke 10:34). Finally, wine is used symbolically of the intoxicating effect of evil (Rev. 14:8, 17:2) and the fierceness of God's wrath (Rev. 14:10, 16:19, and 18:3).

Only one other reference in the New Testament refers to the use of wine (Mark 14:25), and it is in connection with the institution of the Lord's Supper. In this passage Jesus does not use either *oinos* or *gleukos* but simply employs the phrase "fruit of the vine" to denote the contents of the "cup." Since leaven (yeast) was forbidden during the feast of Passover, it is possible that unfermented wine was used. However, the Jewish Talmud indicates that wine mixed with three parts water was to be used for the observance (Pesahim 108 b).

A final note of caution concerning this subject should be added. Wine (*oinos*) is distinguished in the New Testament from strong, intoxicating drinks (*sikera*). John the Baptist abstained from both (Luke 1:15). Others were warned to limit the amount they imbibed (1 Tim. 3:3,8; Tit. 1:7, 2:3).

As far back as Homer (ca. 900 BC), it was the custom to drink wine mixed with water (Liddell and Scott). According to Plutarch, anyone who drank pure wine without any admixture of water was considered a barbarian (*Symposiacs* 3.9). In New Testament times it appears that the general practice was to mix wine with water before consumption, and the normal mixture was three parts water to one part wine. (For additional information on this subject see Robert H. Stein, "Wine-Drinking in New Testament Times," *Christianity Today,* June 20, 1975.) It is also abundantly clear that people who drank wine in this fashion did not drink wine in order to get drunk, but because it was a much safer beverage to drink than the water.

31

The Spirit's Filling

Reference is made several times in Acts to the "filling of the Holy Spirit." In five passages a form of the verb *pimplemi,* denoting the action to be "filled" with the Holy Spirit, is found. Its first appearance is in Acts 2:4. On the Day of Pentecost all of the disciples were "filled with the Holy Spirit." When Peter was before the Sanhedrin, Luke records that Peter, "filled with the Holy Spirit," began to preach to them (Acts 4:8).

In Acts 4:31 a third instance is described. The Christians were together in a private place, "And when they had prayed . . . they were all filled with the Holy Spirit." The fourth occurrence of *pimplemi* is in connection with the experience of Paul at his conversion (Acts 9:17ff.), and the final occurrence is in Acts 13:9 when Paul and Barnabas were opposed by Elymas, the magician. Paul was "filled" on both of these occasions.

The word *pleroō,* a synonym of *pimplemi,* is used only once in Acts to refer to the "filling" of the Spirit. In Acts 13:52 it is employed in the imperfect tense to denote the fact that the disciples were *continually filled* with joy and with the Holy Spirit.

In addition to the times in Acts when the word "filled" is used in verb form, there are three passages in which the adjective *plereis* is found. Acts 6:3, speaking of the first deacons, demands the qualification: "full of the Spirit." When the adjective is used in this manner to describe a person, it means one who is constantly characterized by being filled with the Spirit. This was a part of his character.

Acts 6:5 adds, "They chose Stephen, a man full of faith and of the Holy Spirit." At his martyrdom this quality is echoed again (Acts 7:55): "But being full of the Holy Spirit, he gazed intently into heaven and saw the glory of God, and Jesus standing at the right hand of God." These statements do not mean that Stephen was perfect, but they do indicate that he was consistent in his commitment to Christ.

The only other person in Acts described in this manner is Barnabas (Acts 11:24). Barnabas was a pastor of the church at Antioch, and it is recorded about him, "He was a good man, and full of the Holy Spirit and of faith." Because of his character, "considerable numbers were brought to the Lord."

The Greek root words involved are *pimplemi* and *pleroō,* which have the same three basic meanings. The first meaning is "to fill or make full," as one would fill a waterpot or a container with water. It means filled to the brim.

The second meaning is "to complete or accomplish." These are synonyms of the word "fulfill," which is the same as saying "fill full." The word is used in this manner in Luke 2:6, which says, "Mary's days were fulfilled that she should be delivered." Clearly, this translation does not fit in the context of the filling of the Holy Spirit. The third meaning of this word is "to wholly take possession of a person's mind" or "to come under the complete influence of some person or some idea."

When someone is "filled" with the Holy Spirit, which one of these meanings should be used? There are some who favor the first interpretation. This is evidenced by the common request made to God, "Lord, give me more of your Spirit." However, there are grave problems with thinking of the "filling of the Holy Spirit" in the same terms as water filling a waterpot; one cannot measure the Spirit of God in quantities such as ounces, quarts, or gallons. Moreover, if a person has any of the Holy Spirit, he has enough of the Spirit because the Spirit is omnipotent.

The second translation (fulfill or accomplish) has already been eliminated since it does not fit in this context. The third alternative, "to come under the complete influence of some person," is clearly indicated in at least one passage and appears to be the best choice in all the instances where this phrase is used.

In Ephesians 5:18, Paul draws a contrast between a man drinking wine and a man being filled (*pleroō*) with the Spirit. If a man has had too much alcohol, it is said that he is drunk, inebriated, or *under the influence of alcohol.* He does not behave as he normally does. Instead of being under the influence of alcohol, believers are to be under the influence of the Holy Spirit. When the Holy Spirit takes control of a life, that life will not be the same, and that is good. This is what is meant by being "filled" with the Holy Spirit: to be under the complete control of the Holy Spirit, so He directs one's entire life.

32
Fornication or Adultery?

The Greek word *porneia,* which is usually translated fornication, has been the subject of a great deal of discussion, especially in modern times. The reason for this discussion has been the varied ways it may be understood, and especially because of its bearing on the subject of divorce.

One cause for the lack of clear understanding of the word is: it is rarely used in classical Greek, so it has little background before New Testament times. Originally, it referred to both prostitution and fornication; later it was applied more generally to any unlawful sexual intercourse (Moulton and Milligan).

In the Old and New Testaments *porneia* is used metaphorically to denote: (1.) the worship of idols (Hos. 1:2) or (2.) the assimilation of pagan idolatry and doctrine into the Christian faith (Rev. 14:8, 17:2,4, 18:3, 19:2). As in former times, *porneia* also seems to be used as a general word to include any illicit sexual activity (Rom. 1:29; Acts 15:20,29; Eph. 5:3). On the other hand, in the New Testament *porneia* often has a more specific meaning, distinct from that of *moicheia* (adultery).

In these cases it would more properly be translated premarital sex or sex outside of marriage. An example of this use is found in 1 Corinthians 7:2, where Paul tells the Corinthians that in order to avoid *porneia* (premarital sex), "Let every man have his own wife, and let every woman have her own husband." Other examples of this use are found in Matthew 15:19, Mark 7:21, and Galatians 5:19.

Finally, *porneia* has a fourth application in the New Testament. In 1 Corinthians 5:1, it refers to a case of incest. A man in that church had a continuing relationship with his father's wife (probably his stepmother). Lightfoot, in his *Notes on Epistles of St. Paul,* sums up the situation: (1) it was a lasting relationship (denoted by the present tense); (2) his father was still living (2 Cor. 7:12); (3) divorce or separation is implied because *porneia,* not *moicheia,* is used; and (4) the woman was not a Christian—he is censured and she is not.

Although the passages mentioned above provide a background for the understanding of *porneia,* the debate over the meaning of the word does not center around any of the passages mentioned. The problem arises over Jesus' use of the word in connection with the grounds for divorce.

In Matthew 5:32, Jesus says that a man who divorces his wife, "except for *porneia,* causes her to commit adultery"; and in Matthew 19:9, the statement is expanded to say, "Whosoever shall put away his wife, except it be for *porneia,* and shall marry another, commits adultery (*moichao*); and whosoever marries her which is put away commits adultery (moichao)." The question is: which of the meanings mentioned above applies here?

There is general agreement that Jesus was not using the term metaphorically to refer to spiritual fornication (idolatry). The most popular interpretation is that Jesus was using the word in its general sense to refer to any kind of moral impurity, including adultery. However, there are some factors which seem to rule out this view:

(1) Nowhere else in the New Testament is adultery listed as grounds for divorce; in fact Romans 7:3 seems to rule it out.

(2) While Jesus' statement on divorce is repeated in Mark 10:1-12 and Luke 16:18, the phrase "except for *porneia*"is omitted, indicating that the phrase may have a special meaning related to the context of Jewish life, since Matthew was written to Jews.

(3) The only other use of *porneia* in Matthew is one in which it is contrasted with adultery (*moicheia*—Matt. 15:19). The verb form of *moicheia*is also used in the passages in question and clearly refers to adultery.

(4) The reaction of the disciples indicates that they thought Jesus' position was harsh (Matt. 19:10-11). If He meant adultery, He would be agreeing with the position of Rabbi Shammai—a position which many Jews already held, so why would they show surprise?

(5) There is no instance in the New Testament where *porneia* specifically refers to adultery.

(6) The scriptural attitude is to love one's wife even if she is unfaithful rather than use it as an excuse for divorce (Hos. 3:1-3).

If adultery is ruled out as the proper meaning, to what then might *porneia* refer? If it does not refer to adultery, it must have reference to premarital sex. The question might be asked then, why would divorce be necessary if this immorality happened before marriage? One should be reminded that the Jews practiced betrothal before marriage. This was a legally binding agreement which could only be broken by divorce. Jesus may have meant that if unfaithfulness occurred before the marriage was consummated, then it could be cancelled. Today, one would call this an annulment rather than divorce.

In addition, there is another possible interpretation. The possibility remains that Jesus may have been making reference to incest as the only cause for divorce. The law forbade marriages between those of close kin (Lev. 18). If one takes this as the proper interpretation of Jesus' words, the only marriage which should be ended by divorce is one that was forbidden by the law in the first place: an incestuous one.

So, what is the conclusion of this question? Since the meaning of *porneia* in Jesus' statements in Matthew are not certain, one should compare these passages with the teaching of the rest of Scripture on this subject before he makes a final decision. One must be careful not to take for granted that adultery is grounds for divorce when *porneia* has several other meanings.

The principle of Scripture in this case is: when in doubt, don't. Since *porneia* is a questionable basis for divorce, one is taking the risk of disobeying God by doing so.

33

Demonized

Another of the words which seems to have been redefined during New Testament times is *daimonizomai,* which is translated "to be possessed of a demon" or "to act under the control of a demon." Moulton and Milligan state that in the New Testament sense it seems to occur only in later Greek.

In classical Greek a similar word (*daimonaō*) was used in reference to those who were insane (Xenophon, *Memorabilia* 1.1.9). Thayer defines those "possessed ones" in the New Testament as "persons afflicted with especially severe diseases, either bodily or mental . . . whose bodies, in the opinion of the Jews, demons had entered, and so held possession of them as not only to afflict them with ills, but also to dethrone the reason and take its place themselves; accordingly the possessed were want to express the mind and consciousness of the demons dwelling in them."

While the description given by Thayer of those possessed by demons or "demonized" is well stated, it is unfortunate that he implies these people may simply have been the physically or mentally sick, and the people of those days *attributed* the cause to demons. However, these cases appear to have been real, not imagined. This is evidenced by the demons actually speaking (Luke 8:28ff.) and by the remarkable changes in the people who were relieved of their oppressors, not to mention the fact that Jesus Himself cast out demons on several occasions.

When the uses of *daimonizomai* in the New Testament are examined (Matt. 4:24, 8:16,28,33, 9:32, 12:22, 15:22; Mark. 1:32,

5:15,16,18; Luke 8:28,36, and John 10:21), several facts are apparent. First, not all sickness is attributed to demons. In Mark 1:32, for example, the Greek text makes it clear that the sick and the demon possessed are definitely not the same people. They brought to Jesus "all that were diseased, and them that were possessed with demons." Second, however, some illness is demon related and therefore can be cured only by spiritual means. Third, there is no example of a believer who is possessed. All of those cleansed seem not to have known Jesus previously. Fourth, there appears to be an antithesis between demon possession and the filling of the Holy Spirit. If this be the case, demon possession is not a situation which merely happens but is the result of definite choices one has made.

Finally, one must conclude that New Testament believers were not bound by fear of demons. Kittel observes concerning New Testament faith, "All fear of demons necessarily yields to steadfast assurance." As the Scripture says, "Greater is He that is in you, than He that is in the world" (1 John 4:4).

34

Envy

The word "envy" is often used as a synonym of the word "jealousy" in English usage. As a result, in the King James Version not only is the Greek word *phthonos* rendered "envy," but the word *zelos* (jealousy) is sometimes translated "envy" as well (Acts 13:45; Rom. 13:13; 1 Cor. 3:3; 2 Cor. 12:20; and James 3:14,16). However, while the English terms may at times overlap, the two Greek words have distinctly different connotations.

The word *zelos* is often used in a good sense both in classical Greek and in the New Testament. It may refer to a "zeal, ardor in pursuing or defending something" or to a "fierceness of indignation" (Rom. 10:2; John 2:17; 2 Cor. 9:2). Aristotle uses the word exclusively in this nobler sense "as that active emulation which grieves, not that another has the good, but that itself has it not; and which, not pausing here, seeks to supply the deficiencies which it finds in itself" (Trench). In other words, *zelos* may cause a person to work harder in order to equal what others have done and therefore cause him to improve himself.

Yet, "it is only too easy for this zeal and honorable rivalry to degenerate into a meaner passion" (Trench). Strife is often the result in this case because "those who together aim at the same object, who are thus competitors," are "in danger of being enemies as well" (Trench). In the New Testament, *zelos* is more often used to denote this contentious rivalry or jealousy (Acts 5:17, 13:45; Rom. 13:13; 2 Cor. 12:20; and Gal. 5:20).

In contrast to *zelos, phthonos* is always used with an evil significance; it is incapable of good. It does not denote a desire to have what someone else has (as *zelos* does), but to be sorry that he has it. It is a meaner sin because it does not motivate one to improve himself but only to bring others down to a lower level.

Aristotle put it this way, "They think that every one else is getting what belongs to them"; they feel pain not because they desire something, "but because the other persons have it." But tragically, the envier "has no impulse to raise himself to the level of whom he envies, but only to depress the envied to his own" (*Rhetoric* 2.10). The envier is "sick of a strange disease, another's health" (see Trench).

35

Baptize

The word *baptize* is not native to the English language. Rather, it has been borrowed from Greek. It was simply transposed (transliterated) into the English Bible without translation in order to avoid controversy. In order to find its correct meaning, one must explore the usage of the word in its original setting, Greek literature.

Baptizō, the form of the word generally found in the New Testament, is a later form of the word *baptō* (which has the same basic meaning) and is rarely used in classical Greek (Trench). However, the uses which have been found clearly illustrate the meaning of the word. Arndt uses the following words to describe its meaning: dip, immerse, wash, plunge, sink, drench, overwhelm. Examples of the use of *baptizō* include these: (1) To sink a ship was described as baptizing it (Polybius 2.51.6). (2) It refers to sinking into sleep or intoxication (Kittel). (3) Plato uses the word to describe someone drowning himself in wine (*Symposiacs* 176 B). (4) Metaphorically, *baptizo* is used to describe someone who is over head and ears in debt (Plutarch, *Galba* 21); someone who is drowned with questions (see Liddell and Scott); and the crowds who flooded into Jerusalem during the Roman seige (Josephus, *Jewish Wars* 4.3.3.). (5) Finally, *baptizō* describes the act of drawing water from a vessel by dipping a cup in it (Plutarch, *Alexander* 67).

The sister word *baptō* is also used to refer to the sailing of a ship and the drawing of water by dipping the cup or bucket. Other interesting uses of *baptō* include the dipping of a red-hot iron in water to temper it (tempered iron was "baptized" iron—Homer's *Odyssey* 9.392) and the dipping of clothes in dye to color them (Plato, *Republic* 4.429 D).

In the Septuagint, both words are used with the meaning "to dip." *Baptō* is used in Joshua 3:15 ("the feet of the priests that bore the ark were dipped in the brim of the water"). *Baptizō* is the word used in connection with Naaman's seven-fold dipping of himself in the Jordan River (2 Kings 5:14). That *baptizō* did not mean "sprinkle" is clear from the Greek version of Leviticus 4:6: "And the priest shall dip (*baptizō*) his finger in the blood, and sprinkle (*rantizō*) of the blood seven times before the Lord." Other examples of the use of these words are found in Leviticus 4:17 and 11:32.

In the New Testament these two words (*baptō* and *baptizō*) have several different applications. (1) *Baptizō* refers to the ceremonial ablutions (washings) of the Jews (Mark 7:4; Luke 11:-38). (2) The second usage has the classical meaning, "to dip." In Luke 16:24 the rich man requested that Lazarus dip (baptize) the tip of his finger in water and cool his tongue. The act of Christian baptism, as well as John's baptism, also has this meaning: to dip or submerge in water (1 Cor. 1:14ff; Matt. 3:16; Acts 2:38,41, 8:12,13,16,36-38, 9:18, 10:47-48, 16:15,33, 18:8, 19:5, 22:16). (3) In addition to the literal sense in these passages, *baptizō* is used to denote the baptism of the Holy Spirit. Wuest includes the passage in Romans 6:3-4 ("baptized into Christ") under this category. He says, "The word refers to the introduction or placing of a person or thing into a new environment or into union with something else so as to alter its condition or its relationship to its previous environment or condition." And just as the blacksmith dipped hot iron into water, or the textile worker dipped cloth in the dye for the purpose of dying it, the Holy Spirit joins us to Christ and His body (1 Cor. 12:13), which both "alters our condition" as well as our relationship. (4) Finally, there is the metaphorical use of the word. Jesus speaks of his coming suffering and death as his baptism (Mark 10:38); suffering and death would "overwhelm" Him temporarily. Paul says that the children of Israel were "baptized unto

Moses in the cloud and in the sea" (1 Cor. 10:2). The *Expositor's Greek Testament* explains this reference in this manner:

> "The cloud" shading and guiding the Israelites from above, and "the sea" making a path for them through its midst and drowning their enemies behind them, were glorious signs to "our fathers" of God's salvation . . . Thus "they all received their baptism *unto Moses* in the cloud and in the sea," since in this act they committed themselves to the guidance of Moses, entering through him into acknowledged fellowship with God.

In conclusion, baptism in the New Testament means "to dip or immerse." It never means "to sprinkle." To translate it with the word "sprinkle" not only betrays its true meaning but also causes one to miss the deep, underlying truths which it symbolizes: death to the old life and new life in Christ (Rom. 6:4), new union with Christ (Rom. 6:3), union with the body of Christ (1 Cor. 12:13), and cleansing from sin (Acts 22:16).

36
Decently and in Order

The apostle Paul has a discussion in 1 Corinthians concerning the use of spiritual gifts (and tongues in particular) in the meetings of the church. He closes this discussion with the comment, "Let all things be done decently and in order" (1 Cor. 14:40).

The word for "decently" is *euschemonos,* an adverb, which is a combination of two words: *eu* (well) and *schema* (form or figure). From this literal meaning of "good form," it came to mean "gracefully, becomingly, in a seemly manner." In Romans 13:13, it is translated "honestly" but should include more than that; it refers to proper behavior for a Christian in contrast to the wild, uncontrolled, drunken excesses of pagan society.

In 1 Thessalonians 4:12, believers are told to walk *euschemonos.* Laziness and depending on others to take care of one's needs is not "proper behavior." The adjectival form of the word appears in 1 Corinthians 12:23, where the "comely or becoming" parts of the body are contrasted with the "less honorable." In the context of 1 Corinthians 14:40, it means to behave with "grace and dignity" in contrast to the disorder which had prevailed in the Corinthians' worship.

The second part of the command is given in two words: *kata taxis* (according to order). In Greek literature *taxis* primarily refers to the orderly arrangement of troops or ships in a battle. Thucydides, Herodotus, and Zenophon all often use it in this manner (see Liddell and Scott for references on this use). Similarly, it may refer to a single line of soldiers or a whole division of an army (Herodotus, *The History* 6.111; Thucydides, *The Peloponnesian War* 4.93; 5.68). Another interesting use of the word is in reference to an arrangement with creditors for the paying of a debt (Plato, *Laws* 8.844B).

In the New Testament it is employed with the same basic meaning. Luke 1:8 uses the word to refer to Zechariah's service at the Temple which was according to a "fixed succession observing also a fixed time" (Thayer). It occurs again in Colossians 2:5 when it seems to refer back to the classical usage of a military formation. Even though the Colossians were under attack, their order (military line) was not broken by the enemy.

Finally, it must be noted that belonging to a certain order or military group began to give a person a certain reputation. One was known by the character, quality, and style of the group to which he belonged. For example, Jesus was spoken of as a priest according to the *taxis* of Melchizedek rather than that of Aaron (Heb. 5:6,10, 6:20, and 7:11,17). In 1 Corinthians 14:40, *taxis* seems to relate to the fact that the worship of the church must be carried on in an orderly manner, one that is becoming (*euschemonos*), because a church gets a reputation according to the quality, manner, and "appearance" (Arndt) of its worship.

37

Compassion

The apostle Paul says in Philippians 1:8, "For God is my record how I long after you all in the bowels of Jesus Christ." The Greek work for "bowels" is *splanchnois.* The word literally refers to the inward parts, such as the heart, lungs, liver, and upper intestines.

However, the word seems always to have been used in a figurative sense as well. The Greeks regarded the *splanchna* as the "seat of the more violent passions, such as anger and love" (Thayer). The Hebrews, on the other hand, considered the bowels to be the source of the more tender affections such as kindness, mercy, and compassion (see 1 John 3:17). Paul seems to use the Hebrew concept of the word; therefore, what he is saying to the Philippians is, "I yearn for you all with the *compassion* (affection) that Jesus himself has for you."

The verb form of the word is *splanchnizesthai,* "to be moved with compassion." Barclay observes concerning it, "In the New Testament the word never occurs outside the Synoptic Gospels; and except for three occurrences in the parables it is always used of Jesus."[7] In these parables, those who were examples of compassion were also examples of what God is like and, therefore, what He wants us to emulate. The examples include the master who had compassion on the servant who could not pay his debt (Matt. 18:27), the father of the prodigal son (Luke 15:20), and the Good Samaritan who had compassion on the wounded man (Luke 10:-33).

Concerning Jesus it is written that He was moved with compassion (to the very depths of His being) for the crowd because they wandered as sheep without a shepherd (Matt. 9:36; Mark 6:34). He was moved with compassion for those who were suffering physically—the hungry (Matt. 14:14) and the blind (Matt. 20:34). Finally, He had compassion on those burdened with sorrow such as the widow of Nain who had lost her only son (Luke 7:13).

The most remarkable aspect about this description of Jesus is the glaring contrast between Him and the ideas that pagans held about God. The Stoics taught that God was apathetic, that He did not care about the sufferings of mankind, and if a man wanted to be like God, he must also teach himself not to care. Epictetus even wrote about how a man can train himself to be so uncaring. He must begin with something small, then "proceed to a suit of clothes, a dog, a horse, an estate"; from there he must go on to "self, body, parts of the body, children, wife, brothers" (*Discourses* 4.1.13). He must learn to say, "It doesn't matter; I don't care" (Barclay).[8]

This is one of the reasons why the pagan world was so shocked with the message of the gospel. To them it was incredible not only that did God care, but He cared deeply in His inmost being. He cared enough to become involved in the lives of humans and rescue them from their degraded condition through the death of His Son. *That* is the ultimate example of being *"moved* with compassion."

38

Righteous

In Greek literature the adjective *dikaios* (righteous) had a variety of uses. Its primary uses denote: (1) one who is observant of custom or rule, especially of social rule, one who has a well-ordered life as opposed to one who is ill-mannered or rude; (2) one who is fair and impartial in his judgments; (3) that which is right, lawful, or just, such as a lawful claim, or a man receiving his just deserts; and (4) one who is legally exact or precise in his dealings.

Similarly, *dikaios* (righteous) is used in several different ways in the New Testament:

(1.) It refers to God as the "righteous" judge, the one who declares or pronounces someone righteous. The emphasis here is the fact that God is fair and impartial in His judgment. John says, "Since you know that He is righteous, you know that everyone who does righteousness is born of Him" (John 2:29).

(2.) *Dikaios* is also used to describe Jesus, who is a perfect example of righteousness. Several times He is called the righteous one (Acts 7:52; Matt. 27:19; 1 John 2:1, 3:7). He is the only one who ever lived a life perfectly ordered according to the will of God.

(3.) When it is applied to men, *dikaios* has two meanings: it refers to one who is upright or virtuous and keeps the commands of God (Matt. 13:17; Heb. 12:23). It describes one who is wholly conformed to the will of God. However, in the fullest sense of the word only Jesus can be called righteous ("There is none righteous," Rom. 3:10). In addition, *dikaios* has a legal aspect. It describes a

95

man who is innocent or guiltless according to the law (Matt. 27:19,-24; Luke 23:47).

These two senses are combined in the New Testament when those who are neither upright nor guiltless are declared both righteous and not guilty before God. This is done on the basis of Jesus' sacrifice on our behalf: "By the obedience of one shall many be made righteous" (Rom. 5:19).

39

The Coming of the Lord

In 1 Thessalonians 4:15, Paul uses the phrase, "those who are alive and remain unto the coming [*parousía*] of the Lord." This word translated "coming" literally means "being" (*ousia*) "with" (para). It denotes an "arrival" as well as a "presence with."

Moulton and Milligan cite many references from secular papyrus documents which amply illustrate this usage. In one ancient document a man writes, "The repair of what has been swept away by the river requires my *presence.*" Another writes to his brothers, "We await your *presence.*" In yet another document a woman declares that her husband "swore in the *presence* of the bishops and of his own brothers, 'Henceforward I will not hide all my keys from her.'"

What is more interesting to us, however, is the fact that from the time of the Ptolemies (early third century BC), the word's usage could be a technical expression for the royal "visit" of a king or other persons with great authority. The visit of the king to a city was a heralded event in ancient times. Huge celebrations were planned and elaborate gifts prepared for the visitor. Taxes were often raised to cover these expenses. In the third century BC, taxes were levied to present Ptolemy Soter a golden crown. Wuest mentions another papyrus, "found among the wrappings of a mummy of a sacred crocodile," which speaks of the requisition of grain to help cover the expenses of the *"parousia* of a king."

A second result of the coming of a monarch was the practice of counting time from that date. It was an epoch-making event. Cos dated time beginning anew from the *parousia* of Gaius Caesar in 4 AD. Greece did the same after the visit of Hadrian in 124 A.D.

A third common practice was the minting of advent coins, which commemorated such a visit to a city or province. Hadrian seemed to love this kind of honor, for his travels can be followed and documented by the trail of new coins minted (Barclay).[9]

Barclay lists two other uses of the word in this regard: (1) to mark the invasion of a province by a new conquering power, such as the invasion of Asia by Mithradates; and (2) to celebrate what was considered the visitation of a god, such as when someone was healed at the temple of Aesculapius.[10]

Finally, the coming of the king was an occasion to lay one's grievances before the ruler. In 163-2 BC the Serapeum Twins used the visit of Ptolemy Philometer and Queen Cleopatra to Memphis to air their grievances.

In the New Testament *parousia* describes the presence or the arrival of persons other than the Lord. For instance, Paul says he is glad because of the *"parousia* of Stephanus, Fortunatus, and Achaicus" (1 Cor. 16:17). Later he was comforted by the *"parousia* of Titus" (2 Cor. 7:6). The Corinthians said about Paul that "his bodily *parousia* [presence] was weak" (2 Cor. 10:10). Less common uses of the word include a reference to the "coming" of the lawless one, the antichrist (2 Thess. 2:9), and the "coming of the day of God" (2 Peter 3:12).

From the evidence available, one fact seems clear: the first-century Christians were well aware of the word's technical meaning. Therefore, *parousia* became the word generally used to described the second coming of Christ. It is used by Matthew: "What shall be the sign of thy *coming,* and of the end of the world?" (Matt. 24:3, see also verses 37 and 39). It is used by Paul: "Now we beseech you, brethren, by the *coming* of our Lord Jesus Christ" (2 Thess. 2:1; see also 1 Cor. 15:23, 1 Thess. 2:19, 3:13, 4:15, 5:23; and 2 Thess. 2:8). It is used by James: "The *coming* of the Lord draweth nigh (James 5:7-8). It is used by Peter: "Where is the promise of his coming?" (2 Pet. 3:4). Finally, it is used by John as he exhorts believers to abide in Christ so they may "not be ashamed before him at his *coming"* (1 John 2:28).

Since this word was commonly used by the writers of the Scriptures, what picture did it present to the minds of the early believers? Just as the pagan idea of a *parousia* did, the word suggested an epoch-making event. Jesus would invade the world and conquer the forces of evil. A new era would begin, which would be a time of tremendous celebration for His followers. It signified to them the coming of God Himself to the earth, and it demanded that they prepare so they would not be ashamed because they were not ready for His coming. The word *parousia* is the expression of Zechariah 9:9, "Behold, thy king cometh unto thee" (Deissman).

40

Heresy

Heresy (*hairesis*) is an example, like many others, of a word which has been adapted from classical Greek to fit the unique context of the New Testament. In classical Greek, one of the earliest uses of the word denotes the capture of a city, "a taking" (Herodotus, *History* 4:1; 9:3). The most common meaning assigned to the word in classical times, however, is "a choosing," "a choice," or the "thing chosen."

Thayer calls it "a chosen course of thought and action" or "one's chosen opinion, tenet." In accordance with this idea of choosing, one of the more common uses of the word in Greek papyri documents is in wills. One such document, cited by Moulton and Milligan, begins with the words, "according to the disposition (heresy) below written." A later document uses *hairesis* to denote a bid at an auction.

The word was also used from classical times to denote those who had chosen to follow the same philosophic principles, a school, or sect (Liddell and Scott), although this is a minor usage for that era. In the Septuagint the idea of choice is also present. *Hairesis* refers to a "freewill" offering in Leviticus 22:18.

In the New Testament the most common use of *hairesis* is in reference to a sect or faction. W. E. Vine says that a "sect is a division developed and brought to an issue." It may denote a strong emphasis on a particular truth or set of truths: the sect of the Sadducess (Acts 5:17) or the Pharisees (Acts 15:5, 26:5); or it may denote what is considered to be a perversion of truth: Paul was accused by the Jews of being "a mover of sedition" and a "ringleader of the *Sect* of the Nazarenes" (Acts 24:5; see also Acts 28:22).

The most well-known translation of *hairesis,* however, is "heresy." Its connotation in the New Testament is, in most cases, bad. Peter speaks of teachers who bring in "damnable [destructive] heresies" (2 Pet. 2:1). Paul refers to heresy as one of the evidences of living according to the flesh (Gal. 5:20). In 1 Corinthians 11:19 Paul connects heresy with schisms. He has heard that there are divisions in the church and adds that there must also be heresies. The two go together, as one commentator has observed: "Heresy and Schism are not indeed the same, but yet they constitute merely the different manifestations of one and the same disease. Heresy is theoretic schism; schism is practical heresy" (see Trench).

Let us remember that the Jews called the early Christians heretics (Acts 24:14) and accused them of creating division in the ranks of Judaism, while the Christians were convinced that they were merely preaching the truth. How then does one identify a heretic? From the Christian viewpoint one is guilty of heresy if he chooses to hold to a doctrine or position which is contrary to the Scriptures, the objective standard in such matters (see Barclay on Gal. 5:20).[11]

What is to be done with a heretic? Titus 3:10 gives the answer to that question. Innocent, writing to Jerome in the year 417, comments on this verse:

> Heretics should be admonished once or twice in the beginning
> of heresy and not subjected to a long series of rebukes. When
> this rule is negligently observed, the evil to be guarded against
> so far from being evaded is rather intensified.

41

Tested and Approved

In Philippians 1:10, Paul prays for the saints that they may learn to "approve the things that are excellent" or the "things which differ." The Greek word for approve (*dokimadzō*) has also been translated "prove" (Rom. 12:2), "try" (1 John 4:1), "examine" (1 Cor. 11:28), "discern" (Luke 12:56), "like" (Rom. 1:28), and "allow" (Rom. 14:22).

The primary use of the word in secular literature relates to the testing of metals or coins to ascertain if the metal is genuine or pure. This idea is applied in the New Testament to the believer's works which will be tested by the fire of God's judgment to see if they are genuine (1 Cor. 3:13).

Another meaning for the word is "to recognize as genuine after examination, or to approve." The Athenians used *dokimadzō* to describe a man who had been approved as fit to hold public office or the office of a temple priest (Plato, *Laws* 759 C). This occurred only after careful scrutiny. In the same manner God tested the hearts of Paul and his companions before he entrusted the gospel to them (1 Thess. 2:4). This word is also used in the New Testament in connection with the choosing of deacons (1 Tim. 3:10). They are to be "tried men," those who have not only been tested but who have also stood the test. They should be clearly recognized as genuine.

Finally, God desires that believers test things that differ to determine what is true and what is false, what is to be approved and what is not. We should also be aware that God is testing us! However, *dokimadzō* infers that God's testing is always with the expectation that we are not all dross, but there is some pure metal within us which will be purer than before (Trench).

42
Defense and Confirmation

In Philippians 1:7, Paul declares he is involved "in the defense (*apologia*) and confirmation (*bebaiosis*) of the gospel." The first word, *apologia,* refers to a verbal defense or reply. In secular Greek the verb form meant (1) to give an account of receipts or to recount something at length, or (2) to talk oneself out of difficulty by defending one's actions (Plato, *Gorgias* 480B), and (3) to speak in defense of a fact.

In the New Testament, to make an *apologia* is to defend the gospel against the attacks from outside: from arguments and assaults of the enemies of Christianity (Barclay).[12] First Peter 3:15 says the believer is to "be ready always to give an *apologia* to every man that asks . . ."

In contrast to *apologia* is the word confirmation (*bebaiosis*), which means to make secure or establish. In the secular world the verb form meant: (1) to make sure the possession of a thing (Thucydides, *The Peloponnesian War* 1.122); (2) to establish for oneself, or to secure one's position in argument (Plato, *Theaetetus* 169 E); or (3) to guarantee the title to property one had purchased. According to Liddell and Scott, at Athens it was a legal term for a warranty of title to property sold by a defendant to the plaintiff.

With this background, it is used in the Bible to describe the building up of the gospel from within by increasing the faith and confidence of believers in the gospel. Believers should "establish for themselves" that God's promises are reliable (Rom. 15:8) and make sure that they possess a clear title to the promised inheritance, that salvation is really theirs. When this has been "confirmed" in the believer's heart, then the believer will be ready for the "defense" of the gospel.

43

Perfect

In the Sermon on the Mount Jesus says, "Be ye therefore perfect, even as your Father in heaven is perfect" (Matt. 5:48). Many think this statement means that it is not only desirable but entirely possible for believers to attain an absolute sinless perfection in this life. On the other hand, it is clear that no one, except the Lord Himself, has reached this lofty goal, and it is also certain that one who claims such is deceiving himself (1 John 1:8). What, then, does it mean to be *perfect?*

The Greeks used *teleios* (perfect) in reference to those who are adult, who have "attained the full limits of stature, strength, and mental power within their reach," in contrast to those who are still young men or children (Trench). This sense of the word is found in Hebrews 5:14: "Strong meat is for the full-grown."

The word was also used by the Greeks in an ethical and religious sense. The Stoics contrasted the *teleioi* (mature ones) with those who were still progressing toward the goal. In the mystery religions, it referred to one who had been initiated into the mystic rites. In the New Testament, Paul uses *teleios* to describe spiritually mature persons as opposed to those who are spiritual babes (1 Cor. 2:6, 3:1, 14:20). The same contrast appears again in Ephesians 4:13-14.

Other uses among the Greeks pointed to fulfilled or answered prayers; a person accomplished in a certain field; a sacrifice performed or a sacrificial animal which was "complete"—that is, which met all the ceremonial requirements (see Liddell and Scott for further references). In all of these cases, the idea is that someone (or something) has arrived at a certain standard in a specific area.

Finally, *teleios* was applied by the Greeks to their gods, signifying that they were perfect and omnipotent. In the New Testament it is also applied to God (Matt. 5:48) and His will (Rom. 12:2).

As we try to categorize the usages of *teleios,* a problem becomes evident in understanding its uses. The dilemma lies in the fact that there is a "certain ambiguity" in the word as there is in the English word "perfect"; they are both employed in a relative as well as an absolute sense. Trench observes, "For only so could our Lord have said, 'Be ye therefore perfect (*teleioi*) as your Heavenly Father is perfect (*teleios*).' " The believer shall be made perfect (complete), but not in the same sense that God is perfect—otherwise he would be equal with God.

Paul also shifts from one use to the other in the same passage. He says, "Not as though I had already attained, either were already perfect, but I follow after," (Phil. 3:12) indicating he had not reached the goal as yet. Then he says, "Let *us* therefore, as many as be perfect, be thus minded" (Phil. 3:15). The same word is employed in two different senses. He does admit to having reached a certain spiritual maturity, but not perfection in the sense of having reached the end of spiritual development in his life. He is still pursuing that goal.

Teleios may be translated "full-grown," "adult," "mature," "complete," "finished," or "perfect," depending on the context. Only of God can it be said that He is *teleios* in the absolute sense. Of a person it may be said that he is *teleios,* "fully furnished and firmly established in the knowledge and practice of the things of God . . . not a babe in Christ . . . not always employed in the elements" (see Trench). He is "one who has attained his moral *end,* that for which he was intended, namely to be a man in Christ; however, it may be true that, having reached this, other and higher ends will open out before him, to have Christ formed in him more and more" (Trench).

44

About Bearing Burdens

In Galatians 6:2 Paul writes, "Bear ye one another's burdens, and so fulfill the law of Christ," but then, three verses later he states, "For every man shall bear his own burden." In the English text this appears to be somewhat contradictory, but in the Greek text it is obvious that he is talking about different kinds of burdens.

There are some burdens which the individual must struggle with alone. There are others with which he may need the help of the brethren in Christ. The difficulty lies in knowing when to give aid and when to refrain from it for the burden bearer's own good. It is here that the Greek words give us some direction.

When Paul says, "Bear ye one another's burdens," he makes use of the word *baros*, which denotes "a weight" or "anything which presses on one physically." W. E. Vine defines it as that which "makes a demand on one's resources." This kind of burden may be:

(1) Material—Paul did not want the Thessalonians to bear the financial burden of his support (1 Thess. 2:6). In Jewish literature *baros* was sometimes used to describe the burden of a day's work (Josephus, *Jewish Wars* 1.461);

(2) Spiritual—In Greek literature *baros* referred to a weight of grief or misery, or heavy demands upon a person (Liddell and Scott). In Galatians 6:2 it may refer to a troublesome moral temptation or fault (or the guilt and grief resulting from such a fault), if one concludes that the thought of verse 2 is connected with that

idea in verse 1. If one concludes that verses 1 and 2 are separate statements, then the believer is to help his brother bear any spiritual burden;

(3) Religious—Acts 15:28 refers to the details of the Jewish law as a heavy burden to carry (see also Rev. 2:24);

(4) Metaphorical—The three previous uses are all negative, but the word can be used to describe a positive situation. Paul describes the afflictions the believers must endure now as light compared to the "eternal weight" (*baros*) of our future reward (2 Cor. 4:17).

In Paul's second statement, "Every man shall bear his own burden," the word *phortion* is used instead of *baros*. It means burden or load. Although it has other applications, its primary use in literature is to denote a ship's freight. In fact, the sister word *phortis* is the word for "a cargo ship." It is not surprising, then, to find that Xenophon uses *phortion* for a child being carried in his mother's womb (*Memorabilia* 2.2.5). In comparing these two words for burden, Vine suggests that *phortion* is "something to be borne, without reference to its weight, but *baros* always suggests what is heavy or burdensome." Jesus said, "My burden (*phortion*) is light" (Matt. 11:30), which is in contrast to those who had borne the "burden (*baros*) and heat of the day" (Matt. 20:12).

In the context of Galatians 6:5, *phortion* means that every man must carry his own load, whether heavy or light. Every man has responsibility for the load of work God has called him to do, and no man can take the responsibility for what another is to do. On the other hand, when a brother is burdened down with the weight of sin, of grief, or of calamity, those who are strong should help bear the burdens (*baros*) of the oppressed.

45

Patience

One of the great virtues we often seek after is patience. One may be surprised to find, though, that it is a by-product of the trials and tribulations which we sometimes suffer. James says as much at the outset of his epistle: "Knowing this, that the trying of your faith worketh patience" (James 1:3). Paul gives the same teaching to the Romans: "Knowing that tribulation worketh patience" (Rom. 5:3).

The word translated "patience" is the Greek word *hupomone,* which literally means "to abide under." There is no single English word which conveys all the shades of meaning within *hupomone.* It may mean endurance, fortitude, steadfastness, or perseverance, in addition to patience. In classical Greek it was used to describe: (1) endurance of toil; (2) endurance of grief; (3) steadfastness in the midst of battle; (4) fortitude in the face of coming death (see Barclay); and (5) perhaps the most interesting use—the ability of a plant to live under difficult or unfavorable conditions (Liddell and Scott). In the Inter-Biblical period it was used to describe the power that enabled men to die for God (4 Maccabees 1:11, 9:8).

In the New Testament *hupomone* may be either active or passive (Vine). On the active side, the believer is to have patience or persevere in: (1) well doing (Rom. 2:7), (2) bearing fruit (Luke 8:15), and (3) running the race set before him (Heb. 12:1). On the passive side, the Christian is to be patient in or endure: (1) trials (Rom. 12:12; James 1:12), (2) persecution for the faith (2 Cor.

6:4-5; 2 Tim. 3:10-11), (3) undeserved affliction (1 Pet. 2:20), and (4) the chastening of the Lord (Heb. 12:7).

Trench points out a distinction between *hupomone* (patience) and *makrothumia* (longsuffering) which should be noted. *Makrothumia* expresses patience in respect to persons, while *hupomone* demonstrates patience in respect to things. For this reason, God is never spoken of as having *hupomone*. Trench further observes: "There can be no resistance to God, nor burden upon Him, the Almighty, from things." When God is called the "God of patience" (Rom. 15:5), it is because He gives patience to those who serve Him, not because He is the One who needs it.

Hupomone has as its foundation, courage. "It is the quality which keeps a man on his feet with his face to the wind. It is the virtue which can transmute the hardest trial into glory because beyond the pain it sees the goal" (Barclay).[13] It is the ability to hold out against huge odds. In modern idiom, it describes that ability to "hang in there" when the going gets tough. It is "patient endurance." On the active side, it describes that ability to bloom wherever one is planted, even if it happens to be in the most barren soil.

46

Longsuffering

The word usually translated "longsuffering" is *makrothumia.*
Twelve times it has this translation, although it is translated "patience" on two occasions (Heb. 6:12; James 5:10). Trench calls
makrothumia "a late-developing word." It is not used in classical
Greek at all; it does occur in the Greek Old Testament but does
not have the exact meaning that it has in the New Testament. It
seems to be used in almost the same way as *hupomone* (patience).
First Maccabees describes how the Romans conquered the world
through "patience" (8:4). *Makrothumia* is that persistence which
would never make peace even in defeat (Trench).

In the New Testament the word takes on added significance.
It retains the meaning of earliest Greek in the two passages mentioned, but generally it refers to one's attitude toward other persons. The difference between "longsuffering," as it is used in the
New Testament, and "patience" is explained by J. B. Lightfoot:
"The difference of meaning is best seen in their opposites. While
hupomone is the temper which does not easily succumb under
suffering, *makrothumia* is the self-restraint which does not hastily
retaliate a wrong. The one is opposed to *cowardice* or *despondency,*
the other to *wrath* or *revenge"* (in Colossians 1:11). John Chrysostom's conclusion that "longsuffering" applies to a man who has
powers to avenge himself, yet refrains from the exercise of this
power" is correct, although his comparison of it with "patience"
is faulty (see Trench). Longsuffering is similar in attitude to meekness, which is also "power under control."

The Greeks had no use for this virtue, for to them it was not a virtue at all. Barclay explains, "To the Greek the big man was the man who went all out for vengeance. To the Christian, the big man is the man who, even when he can, refuses to do so."[14]

In the New Testament *makrothumia* describes the attitude of God toward men: "The longsuffering of our Lord is salvation" (2 Pet. 3:15; verb form in 2 Pet. 3:9). The same use is found in 1 Peter 3:20, 1 Timothy 1:16, and Romans 2:4. Next, *makrothumia* is a virtue the minister of the Lord must have in order to be effective in his task. Paul indicates to Timothy that it will take a lot of longsuffering to lead a congregation (2 Tim. 3:10; see also 2 Cor. 6:6 and Titus 2:2).

Finally, *makrothumia* is a characteristic God desires that every Christian have. The fruit of the Spirit includes longsuffering (Gal. 5:22; Eph. 4:2; Col. 1:11, 3:12, and 1 Thess. 5:14). Longsuffering is also included as a characteristic of genuine (*agape*) love (1 Cor. 13:4). A believer, whether a minister or a layperson, must have *makrothumia* if he wants to be like the Lord, because longsuffering is a characteristic of God Himself.

47

Contention and Strife

In two separate lists of vices which characterize the life lived according to the flesh (2 Cor. 12:20, Gal. 5:20), Paul includes the words *eris* (usually translated "strife") and *eritheia* (normally translated "factions" but also translated "strife"). The two words appear to be related because of their similar spelling and meaning; however, most scholars conclude that *eritheia* does not come from *eris*. Barclay, for instance, insists that *eritheia* (also *erithia*) comes from *erithos,* which denotes a "day-laborer" or "hireling." *Eritheia,* then, originally meant "labor for wages."

In classical Greek it referred to farm laborers, such as mowers and reapers, and later to workers with wool (Liddell and Scott). The Greek Old Testament used the word in Isaiah 38:12 with this same meaning.

From this honest beginning the word began to deteriorate in meaning. It came to refer to the "self-seeking pursuit of political office by unfair means" (Arndt). It left the idea of honest labor behind and took up the idea of personal ambition. It serves, but only after asking the question, "What's in it for me?"

In the New Testament *eritheia* refers to self-seeking rivalry between factions who are jockeying for position to gain power in the church. This results in confusion in the church (James 3:16). In addition, it denotes selfish ambition for one's own personal advancement with no regard for others. Paul mentions that certain preachers of the gospel were guilty of this party spirit (*eris*—Phil. 1:15-16) and warned them to denounce personal ambition and vain

114

glory (Phil. 2:3). *Eritheia* also occurs in James 3:14 and Romans 2:8.

The word *eris* refers to strife, quarrel, or debate. In the time of the poet Homer it was used mostly to mean battle-strife. In fact, the Greek goddess Eris was known as the goddess of discord and strife. She excited men to war. After the time of Homer, *eris* came to mean quarreling and disputation of words (Liddell and Scott).

In the New Testament *eris* is used exclusively by Paul. Seven times it is used in connection with envy or jealousy (Rom. 1:29, 13:13; 1 Cor. 3:3; Gal. 5:20; Phil. 1:15; 1 Tim. 6:4; and 2 Cor. 12:20). Only twice is it used without this connection (1 Cor. 1:11 and Titus 3:9). This leads us to conclude that *eris* (strife) also is the result of a self-seeking attitude. Vine says that *eris* is the "expression of enmity" or ill-feeling toward another.

What, then, is the difference between *eris* (strife) and *eritheia* (factions or rivalries)? In the two lists of sins where both are used (Gal. 5:20 and 2 Cor. 12:20), *eris* precedes *eritheia*. This is probably because *eris* is primarily the struggle as a result of enmity between individuals, which, if continued, leads to *eritheia* (factions and rivalries involving groups of people). Both of these words find their roots in selfishness and are connected closely with jealousy and envy (see Ellicott on Gal. 5:20 for his assessment of these words)

48

God Is Not Mocked

(Nose-Thumbing)

In Galatians 6:7, Paul makes a forceful statement: "Be not deceived; God is not mocked; for whatsoever a man soweth, that shall he also reap." The word used for "mock" is *mukterizō,* which means "to sneer at," "to treat with contempt," or "to turn up the nose at."

In Greek literature this term was rare. However, it did occur in both the substantive and verbal form. Its noun form, *muker,* means nose or nostril. It denotes contempt or ridicule. Even in classical times it meant to "turn up one's nose" at someone or something (Moulton and Milligan). In the Septuagint it describes the attitude of Israel toward Jeremiah (Jer. 20:7), the attitude of the wicked toward the advice of Solomon (Prov. 1:30), and the attitude of a foolish man toward his mother (Prov. 15:20).

In the New Testament, *mukerizō* appears only in Galatians 6:7. Another form of the word, with the preposition *ek* added to make it even more intensive, is found in Luke 16:14 (the Pharisees ridiculed Jesus for giving the parable of the unjust steward) and Luke 23:35 (the ruler and people of Israel "derided" Jesus with the words: "He saved others, let Him save Himself"). In addition, there are other words with similar meanings. There is *chleuazō,* which means "to jest about" or "jeer at someone." The Athenians "joked" about Paul at Mars Hill (Acts 17:32). Then there is *dia-chleuazō,* "to scoff at by word or deed." The Jews "scoffed at" the disciples on the day of Pentecost (Acts 2:13).

Finally, there is *empaizō,* whose root meaning is "to play like

116

a child." It is used several times in the Synoptic Gospels, and in all of these references but one it describes those mocking Jesus (Matt. 27:29,31,41; Luke 22:63, 23:11, 23:36). The tragedy of this word is that they "trifled" with Him, "treated Him as a child," and did not take Him as seriously as they should have.

When Paul says, "God is not mocked," he does not mean that men will not try to do so, but that it will not go unpunished. Vine says, "It is impossible to impose on Him who discerns the thoughts and intents of the heart." No one thumbs his nose at God. Just look at what happened to those who tried! (see Matt. 27:25).

49

Have Faith and Be Faithful

To the Philippian jailer, Paul directed, "Believe on the Lord Jesus Christ and thou shalt be saved" (Acts 16:31). The word for "believe" or "have faith" is *pisteuō,* one of the most-used words in the New Testament. For instance, *pisteuō* is found twenty-nine times in the Synoptic Gospels and ninety-nine times in the Gospel of John.

What does it mean to believe? In secular Greek literature, as well as in Scripture, the word has two basic meanings. First, it refers to an intellectual assent or belief that something is true. Thayer calls this meaning the intransitive use of the word: to be sure or be persuaded that something is a fact. This kind of faith does not require any action on the part of the believer—only intellectual acceptance. This type of faith is mentioned in James 2:19: "The demons also believe, and tremble."

The second and more common use of the word in the New Testament is the transitive or active use. It is to "put faith in" or "rely upon" someone or something (Matt. 18:6; John 3:15). An even stronger meaning is often required: "to entrust something to another." Xenophon used *pisteuō* in this manner (*Memorabilia* 4.4.17). This use of the word is found in 2 Timothy 1:12, where Paul says, "I know whom I have *believed* and am persuaded that he is able to keep what I have committed unto him against that day." To believe on the Lord Jesus Christ is more than merely accepting the fact that He is the Messiah, the Savior of the world, but it is to trust in or rely upon Him to save us, to entrust ourselves to His keeping.

Once a person is a believer, a great virtue the Lord desires to find in him is faithfulness. Paul says, "Moreover, it is required in stewards that a man be found faithful" (1 Cor. 4:2). The word for "faithful" (*pistos*) is the adjective form of the verb *pisteuo*. In other words, a man who has faith ought to be faithful.

Like *pisteuō, pistos* has two meanings. First, it can refer to a believing or trusting soul, one who is full of faith. Jesus instructed Thomas to touch His hands and side and, "Be not unbelieving (*apistos*) but believing" (*pistos*—John 20:27). The more common usage of the adjective, however, is in reference to persons (or things) who are faithful or trustworthy. In this sense *pistos* points to God ("God is faithful, through whom you were called," 1 Cor. 1:9; see also 1 Cor. 10:13 and Heb. 2:17) or to persons who have shown themselves as faithful, trustworthy, and true. The Greek poets refer to certain of the Persian monarch's private counselors as the *hoi pistoi* ("the trustworthy ones"—Liddell and Scott). In the New Testament it refers to those who have proved themselves faithful in the transaction of business, the execution of commands, or the discharge of official duties (Thayer). It is used of slaves (Matt. 24:45), stewards (Luke 12:42), and deacons (Eph. 6:21).

Finally, *pistos* refers to things one trusts or relys upon, things which are sure. The primary emphasis here is in reference to someone's words, especially the Word of God. Paul's statement in 1 Timothy 1:15 is called "a faithful saying, and worthy of all acceptation." This same claim is made in 1 Timothy 4:9, 2 Timothy 2:11, and Titus 3:8. In addition, Paul tells Titus that elders of the church should be those who "hold fast to the *faithful* word" which they had been taught (Tit. 1:9). John also testifies that the Lord told him to record the words of Revelation because they were "faithful and true" (21:5, 22:6). The Scripture is spoken of as trustworthy and true, something a person can build his life upon, and the person who does so will have the same characteristics—he will be found faithful.

50
Cheerful Givers

"God loves a cheerful giver" is a famous stewardship statement made by the Apostle Paul to the Corinthians (2 Cor. 9:7). Actually, this is Paul's paraphrase of Proverbs 22:9. He substitutes the verb "loves" for "blesses," which is found in the Greek version of the Old Testament. The same idea is also found in Deuteronomy 15:10: "Thine heart shall not be grieved when thou givest unto him." The Greek words for "cheerful giver" are *hilaros* and *dotes,* neither of which is used anywhere else in the New Testament.

The key word *hilaros* (cheerful) has three different meanings in Greek literature. (1) In classical Greek writings it is used in reference to the gods to signify a propitious attitude (Plato, *Laws* 712B). Vine describes this attitude as "that readiness of mind, that joyfulness, which is prompt to do anything." It describes one who is not only willing, but anxious to help. It is the opposite of one who is reluctant or has to be forced to help (2 Cor. 9:7). (2) Of men it signifies a gracious, kindly, or gentle attitude (Homer, Iliad 9.639). Arndt points out that the word is also used in a similar sense to describe the cooperative attitude of sheep.

(3) Finally, *hilaros* describes a glad, cheerful, or even merry attitude. Plato uses it to denote the frame of mind of a man who has been drinking wine (*Laws* 649A). Moulton and Milligan cite a second- or third-century papyrus document which uses the word to describe a person who is joyful about his salvation. In the Greek Old Testament the verb form *hilarunō* is used in Psalms 104:15 to translate the Hebrew word meaning "to cause to shine"; and the

noun form of the word, translated "cheerfulness," is used in Romans 12:8 in connection with the gift of showing mercy.

The importance of the proper attitude in giving is underscored by a rabbinic saying cited by Barclay: "to receive a friend with a cheerful countenance and to give him nothing is better than to give him everything with a gloomy countenance."[15] This is especially true in reference to God because He does not need anything we might give, but it is we who *need* to give because God loves an enthusiastic (propitious), kind, hilariously radiant donor.

51

Full Assurance

To the Thessalonians Paul wrote, "Our gospel came not unto you in word only, but also in power, and in the Holy Ghost, and in much assurance" (I Thess. 1:5). The word translated "much assurance" is *plerophoria.* This word rarely occurs outside biblical and ecclesiastical sources. In the secular papyri, however, some light is shed on the meaning of the word by the variety of the contexts in which it is used. First, in legal matters it was used to refer to the "accomplishing" or "settling" of an issue in court. Second, it referred both to the collecting of a debt in full and the paying of a debt in full. Finally, it was used to describe an affection which is "fully reciprocated" (Moulton and Milligan).

There are two basic ideas which the word conveys: "fulfilment" or "completion" and "full assurance" or "entire confidence." In the New Testament both meanings are found, although the second one is more common. The first meaning is found in the verb form only. Paul speaks of Epaphrus who labored that the Colossians might be "perfect and *fully complete* in all the will of God" (Col. 4:12). Paul wrote also that the Lord had strengthened him so his preaching might be "fully-completed" (2 Tim. 4:17), and he encouraged Timothy to "completely fulfil" the ministry which God had given him (2 Tim. 4:5).

The second meaning is found in several contexts. First, it is used by Luke in the introduction to his Gospel (Luke 1:1). He says that he is going to set forth a declaration of those things which can be "fully-assured." He is convinced of the accuracy of his facts.

Second, the verse at the beginning of the study (I Thess. 1:5) can be interpreted two ways. When Paul says the gospel came in much assurance he may mean that it was preached to them with deep conviction on the part of the preachers. On the other hand, some see it as a description of the marvelous assurance these believers had that God had saved them. This second meaning is also found in Colossians 2:2 also, where the Scripture speaks of the full assurance which knowledge of the mystery of God's plan can bring.

Third, as believers we are to serve God dilligently with the full confidence that hope gives (Heb. 6:11), draw near to God in the full assurance that faith gives (Heb. 10:22), and live by the convictions of which we have been "fully persuaded" by God (Rom. 14:5). Abraham is a prime example of one who lived such a life of faith because he had "complete confidence" that God would keep his promises (Rom. 4:21).

As believers then, we have a message in which we can have complete trust. We can preach it with conviction, receive it with full assurance, and live it with complete confidence, for in *plerophoria* there is no room for doubt!

52
Work and Labor

In 1 Thessalonians 1:3, Paul says that he is thankful for the "work of faith" and the "labor of love" which the Thessalonians had exhibited. The two words, "work" (*ergon*) and "labor" (*kopos*), are also used together in Revelation 2:2, where the two are followed by the word "patience," as they are in 1 Thessalonians 1:3. Although these two words are similar in meaning, they provide an interesting contrast.

The first word (*ergon*) is very common in the New Testament. It occurs more than twenty-five times in the Gospel of John alone. It refers to "active work," to being occupied with one's business or employment. An example of this use is Acts 13:2 in which Paul and Barnabas are separated by the Spirit for the "work" whereunto God had called them. They were to be occupied with the work of missions. In like manner the Son of man has committed to every one of His servants a specific work (job) to do while He is away.

In addition, *ergon* may refer to the product or result of one's effort. For example, Hebrews 1:10 says, "Thou, Lord, in the beginning hast laid the foundation of the earth; and the heavens are the *works* of thine hands." Finally, *ergon* may speak of an "act" or "deed": a "work." Examples of this use are also plentiful. Paul says, "They profess that they know God; but in works they deny him" (Tit. 1:16), and again, "Not by works of righteousness which we have done, but according to his mercy he saved us" (Tit. 3:5). In conclusion, *ergon* refers to activity which may be easy or even

124

pleasant; it may be either good or bad. It has no further connotation.

In contrast to *ergon* is the second word for work, which is *kopos* (labor, toil). Vine defines *kopos* as "toil resulting in weariness." Trench observes that the emphasis is not so much on the "actual exertion which a man makes" as on the "weariness which follows on this straining of all his powers to the utmost." He also points out that this word is often used for the labors of the Christian ministry, so it contains a warning for all that are engaged in that ministry. For example, Paul called his labors among the Thessalonians *kopos,* and he was fearful that it might be in vain (1 Thess. 3:5; see 1 Thess. 2:9 and 2 Thess. 3:8 also). He instructs the Ephesian elders to labor "to support the weak" (Acts 20:35).

It is also interesting that Jesus, after He had told the disciples to "look on the fields; for they are white already to harvest," tells them they will be reaping the fruit where they had not labored, but He reminds them that others had already labored and they would reap the benefits because of that labor, *kopos* (John 4:35-38).

A second use of *kopos* is found both in secular documents, as well as Scripture. When used in connection with the verb *parechō* (have near), it means "to give someone trouble" or "make work" for them. Moulton and Milligan cite several references from the Greek papyri of the second century. One speaks of a barley harvest: the writer says, "We never had so much trouble in winnowing it." Another says, "With great difficulty I made them set to work at the former rent."

Four times it is used like that in the New Testament. Jesus rebukes the disciples for the "trouble" they gave the women who anointed Him (Matt. 26:10; Mark 14:6). The man with the persistent friend who dropped in at midnight said to him, "Trouble me not" (Luke 11:7), and Paul told the Galatians, "From henceforth let no man trouble me: for I bear in my body the marks of the Lord Jesus" (Gal. 6:17).

In conclusion, both of these words refer to work; however, *Ergon* may mean any kind of work, whether good or evil, pleasant or unpleasant, while *kopos* refers only to that kind of work which is difficult and even wearisome or troublesome.

When Paul commends the Thessalonians for their "work of faith" and "labor of love," he means that they had the kind of faith which caused them to be busy (actively serving) for God and the kind of love which caused them to take on the most difficult tasks for Him.

53

The Word—Part 1

One of the most familiar New Testament words, even to the English reader, is *logos* (word). Trench defines *logos* as "a word, saying, or rational utterance of the *nous* [mind] whether spoken . . . or unspoken." Wuest adds that *logos* refers to "the word or outward form by which the inward thought is expressed and made known" or "the inward thought or reason itself." Most scholars agree with Wuest that *logos* does not refer to "a word in the grammatical sense as the mere name of a thing, but rather the thing referred to." In the New Testament *logos* is used in three different ways.

First, it refers to that which is either spoken or written. Next, it refers to the thought behind what one says. Finally, it refers to the Living Word—it is a title for the Son of God.

The first category is the most common. In referring to speech, *logos* may mean a single word, such as when the centurion said to Jesus, "Speak only a word" (Matt. 8:8), and again, Jesus expelled demons with only one "word" (Matt. 8:16). However, it is fully as common for *logos* to denote what someone has said, such as a whole sermon, rather than a single word (see Trench). In 1 Timothy 5:17 it refers to the "preaching" of the elders. In 1 Thessalonians 1:5 and 2 Thessalonians 2:15 it has reference to speech in general.

In addition it may refer to a question (Matt. 21:24), a prayer (Matt. 28:15), a proverb (John 4:37), or a discourse (Acts 14:12). All of these, however, speak of things which have been spoken.

Moreover, one well-known scholar argues that *Logos* implies only a spoken message and that the Christian message is not that which is learned from books. The word is only communicated through the preaching and sharing of the church; he claims, so it cannot be reduced to the printed page. If this be so, then the Bible could not be called the Word (*logos*) of God.

There are several passages which indicate that this contention is incorrect. In Acts 1:1 Luke refers to the "former book" (*logos*) which he had written. Peter speaks of the "prophetic word" and Scripture as one and the same (1 Pet. 1:19-20). James, the brother of Jesus, also uses *logos* to refer to the words of the prophets "as it has been written" (Acts 15:15). It is clear that the Scripture is also *logos,* the Word of God.

The second use of *logos* points to the thought behind what one says. There are several contexts in which this meaning is found. It refers to the reason or faculty for thought. Paul says to the Ephesian elders, "Neither do I count (*logos*) my life dear unto myself" (Acts 20:24). Another use which involves the mind is in the area of reckoning or settling one's accounts. In Matthew 18:23 Jesus says, "Therefore is the kingdom of heaven likened unto a certain king, which would take account (*logos*) of his servants" (see Phil. 4:15).

A similar use is in reference to the judgment of God. Paul says, "So then everyone of us shall give account (*logos*) of himself to God" (Rom. 14:12). It is used concerning matters before civil courts as well. Luke says, "If Demetrius, and the craftsmen which are with him, have a matter (*logos*) against any man, the law is open" (Acts 19:38). Finally, it may refer to the motive or cause one has behind an action. A good example of this is in Acts where Peter says to Cornelius, "I ask therefore for what intent (*logos*) you have sent for me?" (Acts 10:29).

The final and most important use of *logos* is to denote the Living Word of God. It came to be used as a title for the Son of God, the Personal Word of God, Jesus Christ. The background of this use is varied. By the Greek philosophers this word was used to refer to the Divine Reason (Epictetus 1.3.3) which both put the universe in order and keeps everything in the universe operating in an orderly fashion. For example, Heraclitus called the *logos* the "omnipresent Wisdom by which all things are steered", yet he did not think of the *logos* as a person but as an impersonal force.

The Jews also were fond of the term *logos*. In the Aramaic translation (targums) of the Old Testament, *logos* was one of the words substituted for the name of God in order to avoid using God's name in vain. One of the most striking examples is this: Adam and Eve heard "the voice of the *logos* (the Lord God) walking in the garden" (Gen. 3:8). Moreover, Genesis 28:21 says that Jacob took the *logos* to be his God.

With this information in mind, we must conclude that in the first century wherever targums were used, Jews identified the *logos* with God. Besides the use of *logos* in the targums, the Old Testament itself speaks of the word of God as the agent of God Himself. The word of God is described as doing things. "By the word of his mouth were the heavens made" (Ps. 33:6). Finally, rabbinic teaching also employed the term *logos*. Philo of Alexandria used the term more than 1,300 times in several different ways. One of these was to refer to "God Himself as revealed." One cannot know God's essential being, but His *logos* is His thought revealing Him to men.

When John wrote his Gospel he realized that both Jew and Greek would understand when he called Jesus the *Logos,* that Jesus was the Creator and Sustainer of the universe, that He indeed is God.

54
The Word—Part 2

There is a second word translated "word" in the New Testament. It is *hrema*. Although *hrema* is not as important a concept in the New Testament as *logos*, it is still a commonly used word. Like *logos*, it may refer both to that which is spoken or that which is written. It may refer to one word. For example, Jesus, at His trial, refused to answer Pilate even "a word" (Matt. 27:14). Again, Jesus said that men would be required to give an account of "every idle word" they speak (Matt. 12:36). In the matter of church discipline we are to take a witness that every *word* may be established (Matt. 18:16).

Hrema is also used to refer to an entire sermon or any part of it. Luke 7:1 says, "Now when He had ended all his *sayings* in the audience of the people, he entered into Capernaum."

It is often used to denote the written Word of God or parts of it. It may refer to a prophecy, such as when Jesus spoke to the disciples about His impending death (Luke 18:34). It may denote a command: "At thy *word* I will let down the net" (Luke 5:5). In Luke 2:29 it is used of the promise God gave to Simeon that, before his death, he would see the Messiah.

In addition to these specific uses, *hrema* refers several times to the gospel. It is called the "word which by the gospel is preached to you" (1 Pet. 1:25). It is named the "word of faith, which we preach" (Rom. 10:8) and the word "which was published throughout all Judea" (Acts 10:37). Other occurrences refer to the Word of God in its entirety. First Peter 1:25 says, "The word of the Lord endureth for ever." Jesus says in Matthew 4:4, "Man shall not live by bread alone, but by every word that proceedeth out of the mouth of God."

John also adds Jesus' statement that not only are all of God's words the words of life, but that He had the authority to speak for the Father (John 3:34). The most important statement in this regard, however, is the one made by the Apostle Paul. In Ephesians 6:17, he says that the believer is to take the "sword of the Spirit, which is the word [*hrema*] of God" as his only offensive weapon.

Vines argues that this does not refer to "the whole Bible as such, but to the individual scripture which the Spirit brings to our remembrance for use in time of need." While one may not need to use all of the Word to confront any single problem, it must be maintained that all of the Scripture is always the sword of the Spirit. Neither do individual statements in the Bible *become* the Word of God as they speak to us individually. The *hrema* (the thing spoken) of God is always God's word if it was ever God's word. It is God's word because God spoke it, not because it speaks to us.

Finally, in comparison to *logos, hrema* is an inferior word. It appears that all of the uses of *hrema* mentioned above are paralleled by similar uses of the word *logos*. On the other hand, *logos* has special uses which *hrema* does not have, especially in its reference to the Living Word, Jesus Himself (John 1:1ff.). What, then, is the real difference between the two? *Hrema* refers to the grammatical word itself which is spoken or written. *Logos* is much bigger than that. It includes the concept for which the word stands. It is not merely the name of a person or thing, but the person or thing itself.

55

Forgive

Aphiemi is a verb which is translated by fourteen different words in our English Bible. Its best known translation is the word "forgive." The term is a combination of *apo* (from) and *hiemi* (I send). Moulton and Milligan give examples to show that originally the word meant to "throw." However, there are also examples which demonstrate that before the time of Christ, the word had already begun to be used in its New Testament sense of "forgive." For example, the Rosetta Stone (ca. 196 BC) mentions a total "remission" of taxes. Another interesting example from a later secular papyrus (156 AD) uses the word in the context of leaving a crop unharvested.

In the New Testament *aphiemi* has four distinct but related meanings. First, it means to let go or even to bid someone to depart (send away). When Jesus was on the cross at the point of death, it is recorded that He "dismissed" (*aphiemi*) His Spirit. In this context it cannot mean "forgive." Another example where it is possible to use this translation is in Paul's discussion of marriage (1 Cor. 7:11). The husband is not to let his wife go; here, it may mean he is not to "dismiss" her. However, in 1 Corinthians 7:11, it may also be translated with the second meaning of the word, which is "leave" or "abandon." The "husband is not to abandon his wife." This second meaning is also found in Matthew 26:56 where it is said that Jesus' disciples "*abandoned* him and fled" after His arrest in Gethsemane. (See Rev. 2:4 also).

The third use of *aphiemi* is "to permit" or "to allow." John

the apostle uses this meaning in Revelation 2:20, when he charges
the church at Thyatira with allowing the woman called Jezebel to
teach that idolatry and fornication were permissible for believers
(evidently during gatherings of the church). Jesus also uses *aphiemi*
in His command to the disciples: "Suffer [allow] the little children
to come unto me" (Mark 10:14).

The final meaning of *aphiemi* is to cancel, remit, pardon, or
forgive. It is used to denote the cancelling or forgiving of debts.
Matthew utilized it to describe the forgiving of all a slave's debts
by his lord (Matt. 18:27). It is also used like this in the Lord's
Prayer (Matt. 6:12). More important, however, is its use in the
context of forgiving sin. First John 1:9, for instance, says, "If we
confess our sins he is faithful and just to forgive us our sins." In
addition, John says, "Your sins are forgiven you for his name's
sake" (1 John 2:12). Vine says that *aphiemi* "signifies the remission
of the punishment due to sinful conduct, the deliverance of the
sinner from the penalty Divinely, and therefore righteously, im-
posed." And that is not all, it includes the "complete removal of
the cause of offense" because of the vicarious and propitiatory
death of Christ. Barclay puts it another way: "The whole essence
of the word is the undeserved release of a man from something that
might justly have been inflicted upon him or exacted from
him."[16]

One must agree that the idea behind *aphiemi* is the Old Testament practice of the Year of Jubilee in which slaves were released
and debts were forgiven (Lev. 25; Deut. 15). What was carried out
in a physical manner in their custom is paralleled in the New
Testament in a spiritual manner. The sinner is released from the
clutches of sin and his debt is forgiven his debt. And as Trench
describes it, the "partaker of the *aphesis* has his sins forgiven, so
that unless he bring them back upon himself by new and further
disobedience (Matt. 18:32; 34; 2 Peter 1:9, 2:20), they shall not be
imputed to him, or mentioned against him anymore."

56
Moderation

Paul writes to the Philippians (4:5), "Let your moderation be known unto all men." The word for moderation is *epieikes,* an adjective which is found five times in the New Testament (1 Tim. 3:3; Titus 3:2; James 3:17; 1 Peter 2:18). In addition the noun form is found twice (Acts 24:4; 2 Cor. 10:1).

The problem involved in translating this term is that it has no English equivalent. It has been translated by the terms: clemency, gentleness, graciousness, forbearance, kindness, mildness, fairness, and sweet reasonableness. To illustrate the problem, in the six occurrences of these words in the New Testament, Moffatt uses six different words to translate them. The King James Version uses gentleness or gentle in four instances, but also employs clemency, moderation, and patience. However, none of these terms adequately represent what *epieikes* or *epieikeia* express. Since they cannot be accurately translated, they must be explained.

About *epieikeia* Trench makes this point:

> It expresses exactly that moderation which recognizes the impossibility cleaving to all formal law, of anticipating and providing for all cases that will emerge, and present themselves to it for decision; which, with this, recognizes the danger that ever waits upon the assertion of *legal* rights, lest they should be pushed into *moral* wrongs . . .

It is the quality that "rectifies and redresses the injustices of justice." In effect, it represents true justice as contrasted with legal justice. Aristotle used the word *epieikeia* in reference to that which corrects the law when the law is deficient because of its generality (*Nicomacheon Ethics* 5.10.6). It is possible to be completely legal and yet be unfair or even immoral in one's judgments.

A second point concerning these terms, which Aristotle valued, is that there is a great contrast between the man who is *epieikes* and the man who is *akribodikaios,* "the man who stands up for the last tittle of his legal rights." Barclay is correct when he notes that there is a vast need for the quality which these words describe: "We live in a society where men insist on standing on their legal rights, where they will do only what they are compelled to do, and where they desire to make others do all that they can compel them to do."[17]

The third thought about "moderation" is that the best example of it is God Himself. "All his goings back from the strictness of his rights as against men; all his allowance of their imperfect righteousness, and giving of a value to that which, rigorously estimated, would have none; all his refusals to exact extreme penalties . . . we may contemplate as *epieikeia* upon his part" (Trench). God is always fair, always gracious, and always mild in his actions toward us in comparison to what we deserve. Do not think that *epieikeia* means that God will never be harsh with anyone, because there are times when His very fairness will demand judgment, but He is not anxious to punish the guilty.

What then does Paul mean when he says, "Let your moderation be known unto all men"? He is saying that: (1) as believers we should have a reputation as those who are not simply content to live only by the letter of the law, but to rise above that to live by the fairness and equity intended, though not demanded by it; (2) Christians are not to be characterized as those who are always selfishly demanding their rights but are more concerned with others; (3) believers are to pattern themselves after God Himself because He is the best example of *epieikeia.*

57
Miracles, Wonders, and Signs

In his sermon at Pentecost, Peter declares that Jesus Christ was approved of God "by miracles, and wonders, and signs, which God did by him" (Acts 2:22; these three words are also used together in 2 Cor. 12:12 and 2 Thess. 2:9).

These three words used to describe Jesus' words are *dunamis* (power, in the plural it is used to denote powerful deeds or miracles), *teras* (wonders), and *semeion* (signs). All of these are used to describe the supernatural work of Christ, and as Trench points out, the ancients were fond of drawing distinctions between them. Many of these distinctions will not stand close examination, yet some of them are still passed on today, so it is necessary that they be examined to ascertain what, if any, the real distinctions are.

The first of these words is "miracles" (*dunamis*). It denotes those works which direct the outworking of the mighty power of God. The word is intended to point to the supernatural origin and character of an event. Jesus Himself uses the word to describe His own works in Chorazin and Bethsaida (Luke 10:13).

The second word is *teras* (wonders). Vine says that it refers to something strange, which causes the beholder to marvel or wonder. It is always in the plural, and it is usually accompanied by the plural of the word *semeion* (signs). Trench argues that *teras* is not derived from *treo* (the terrifying), but is connected with tereo (keep); it is "that which for its extraordinary character is wont to be observed and *kept* in the memory." It looks at a miracle as a "startling, imposing, amazement-wakening" event.

Teras refers thirteen times in the New Testament to the wonderful works of God; nine of these are in the Acts (John 4:48; Acts 2:19,22,43, 4:30, 5:12, 6:8; 7:36, 14:3, 15:12; Rom. 15:19; 2 Cor. 12:12; and Heb. 2:4.) However, it should also be noted that three times it is used to describe the "wonders" of Satan. Paul says that the "man of sin" will come "after the working of Satan with all power and signs and lying wonders" (2 Thess. 2:9). Other references to Satan's works are found in Matthew 24:24 and Mark 13:22. The reason that *teras* never occurs by itself, but is always accompanied by the word "sign," is never to let us dwell only on the amazing character of the event itself, but to point us to the person and purpose behind it. Although not all wonders are supernatural in character—that is, they cannot be explained by natural laws—they all point us to someone who is working through them, either God or Satan.

This leads us to the third word Peter used in his sermon to describe the acts of Jesus' ministry, *semeion* (signs). Moulton and Milligan cite examples from secular Greek papyri that demonstrate its background. First, it is used to denote a seal which is intended to be a proof that a letter or package had not been opened before it reached its destination. Second, it referred to an outward distinguishing mark, such as a blemish that would disqualify a man from the Levitical priesthood. Third, it was used of a boundary marker for land. Finally, it was used even in secular society in the New Testament sense of a miracle or wonder.

Perhaps the most relevant of all these in helping us see the purpose of signs in the New Testament is in connection with the first use listed above. Not only would a letter be sealed, but the bearer of the letter was sometimes given something by the sender as proof of his commission. In the same manner the signs that Jesus did served to prove that He was commissioned by the Father to bring salvation to us. In the New Testament, signs were given to verify the authenticity of the Apostles' commission as well. Paul says, "Truly the signs of an apostle were wrought among you in all patience, in signs, and wonders, and mighty deeds" (2 Cor. 12:12).

Not only can a sign in the New Testament be given to confirm one's mission as authentic, but it can be given as a warning or admonition. Jesus told the Jews that they would receive no other sign except the "sign of the prophet Jonah" (Matt. 16:4), which meant unless they accepted His resurrection as genuine, they would miss the salvation of God in the gospel. The most common use of *semeion* is to refer to miraculous acts which are taken of God's authority and power (John 4:54, 10:41, and 20:30). In addition, signs are spoken of as God's "billboards" to alert us to the coming of future events. In Matthew 24:3, the disciples asked for signs, and Jesus gave them several that precede His coming (see also Luke 21:7; Acts 2:19; Rev. 12:1,3, and 15:1). However, like *teras* signs can also be performed by demons (Rev. 16:14) false prophets (Matt. 24:24), and Satan and his agents (Rev. 13:13,14, 19:20; 2 Thess. 2:9).

Although many have attempted to draw distinction between miracles, wonders, and signs as words describing different kinds of events, the New Testament, as well as other Greek sources, seem to use more than one of these terms in reference to the same event. Trench concludes this when he says, "The same miracle is upon one side a *teras,* on another a *semeion,* and the words most often refer, not to different classes of miracles, but to different qualities in the same miracles." When *dunamis* is used the emphasis is upon the source of the power producing the miracle. When *teras* is used it emphasizes the startling effect the miracle had on those who saw it. When *semeion* is used the intention of the writer is not to dwell on the miracle itself but to lead us to something beyond the event.

It is, as Trench says, "a kind of finger-post of God" pointing us to the truth God would have us to learn from it.

58

Form and Fashion

Because it deals with the crucial subject of the person of Jesus Christ, one of the most important passages in the New Testament is Philippians 2:5-11. Two of the key words concerning Jesus and who He is are *morphé,* which is translated "form," and *schema,* which is translated "fashion." Verse six says that Jesus existed in the "form" (*morphé*) of God and then He took on the "form" (*morphe*) of a servant.

Thayer says that the root meaning of the word is "to lay hold of, seize." It originally referred to the external appearance of something which represented to the beholder that which was real and essential in the object. J. B. Lightfoot says that form is "the visible impression and the stamp of the inner being and corresponds thereto." He bases this definition on the use of *morphe* in Plato and later Greek philosophers.

Form is that which can be perceived which accurately conveys the specific character of the person or thing seen. As Wuest puts it, *Morphe* refers to the "outward expression" one gives of himself, that "outward expression proceeding from and being truly representative" of one's inward character and nature. Trench explains correctly that the word implies the Deity of Christ. It does not refer to "being," but "mode of being" or "mode of existence"; however, only God could have the mode of existence of God.

As this passage points out, Jesus, who from eternity had existed "in the form of God," took on the manner of existence of a servant; yet he was not a servant of man, but the servant of Jehovah. "Form of God" includes "the whole nature and essence of Deity, and is inseparable from them, since they could have no actual existence without it" (Vine). Anything which can be separated from "form" is not part of it. It is that essential form which never changes.

In the New Testament, other words related to *morphe* are used several times to describe the inner change which takes place when a person is born again. This "entire change of the inner life . . . is spoken of as a conversion of *morphe* always, of *schema* never" (Lightfoot). It is a change of one's appearance which is based on a change in his essential character, not merely a change in his outward appearance.

The believer is foreordained to be "conformed (*summorphos*) to the image of His Son" (Rom. 8:29). Romans 12:2 commands us to "be not conformed (*suschematizo*) to this age, but to be transformed (*metamorphoo*) by the renewing of the mind." Paul, himself, desired to be "made comfortable (*summorphizo*) to His death (Phil. 3:10). Galatians 4:19 and 2 Corinthians 3:18 also uses forms of *morphe* to describe the change that Christ brings to the inner man.

In two other instances *morphe* and its kindred words are used in reference to Jesus. In describing the transfiguration, the gospel writers say that He was "transfigured before them" (*metamorphoo*, Matt. 17:2, Mark 9:2). This word is used instead of *schema* and its derivations in order to emphasize the magnitude of the change that they witnessed that day. The veil was lifted, and His glory was allowed to shine through before their eyes. They saw more than a change in His outward appearance; they saw a part of His Being that they had never been allowed to see before. They had seen Him with the form of a servant; now they saw the glory He had before He took on that form.

A similar use of the word is found in reference to Jesus' appearance to the disciples after the resurrection (Mark 16:12). It says that He appeared to them "in another form." Lightfoot argues that *morphe* is used here because the writer does not want to give the impression that the resurrection body is only superficial and unreal. However, most evangelical scholars today would discount this reference as a later addition to the text since it does not appear in the earliest manuscripts of the New Testament. One must admit that it is difficult to explain the use of the word in this context if the passage is accepted as genuine.

The contrasting word *schēma,* which is translated "fashion" in Philippians 2:8, refers to the outward appearance and has a superficial character which can be very deceiving. Perhaps the passage in which the use of *schēma* is best demonstrated is 2 Corinthians 11:13-15. Paul says that false apostles attempt to take on the outward appearance of apostles of Christ, Satan transforms himself into an angel of light (the outward appearance only—he cannot change his essence or true character), and Satan's ministers appear as ministers of righteousness. The *schēma* (fashion) of the world is passing away (1 Cor. 7:31), and therefore the believer is told not to be conformed to (take on the outward appearance of) the world, but to be transformed (*metamorphoō*—in the inner man) by having his mind renewed (Rom. 12:2).

So when Paul says that Jesus was "found in fashion (*schēma*) as a man," he was referring to what Jesus was in the eyes of man, the form of his outward existence by which he was recognized as a man. It must be noted that the *schēma* (his outward presentation to the world—that is, his fleshly body) was not part of his *morphē* (his form which is the expression of His essential nature). The *schēma* may change from time to time, but the *morphē* is immutable.

59

Psalms, Hymns, and
Spiritual Songs

The Apostle Paul indicates that one of the results of a life "filled with the Spirit" should be "speaking to yourselves in psalms, hymns, and spiritual songs, singing and making melody in your heart to the Lord" (Eph. 5:18-19). These three words for songs occur again in a similar admonition in Colossians 3:16.

Many expositors in the past have commented on the use of these three words together. Some have stressed the fact that it is possible for the same song to be described by all three words, and they refuse to draw any distinctions between them. One must admit that it is difficult to draw exact differences between them. However, the question must be asked, why does Paul use all three words, when one would suffice, if they all mean the same thing? One must agree with Trench when he writes, "Still each must have had a meaning which belonged to it more, and by a better right, than it belonged to either of the others."

The word *psalmos* originally referred to the striking or plucking the strings of a musical instrument with one's fingers. Later it came to designate a song sung to musical accompaniment, especially that of a harp (see Liddell and Scott). Generally speaking the word psalm in the New Testament refers to one of the psalms found in the Old Testament Book of Psalms. In Acts 13:33 and Luke 24:44, it is used specifically like this, and it is probable that it is used with the same meaning in 1 Corinthians 14:15 and 26.

The second word is *humnos* (hymn). It is generally agreed that a hymn was a song of praise. In Greek pagan literature there were many examples of hymns being sung to the Greek gods or even human heroes such as Alexander The Great. It is interesting that the word *humnos* is not used in any of the writings of the Apostolic Fathers and appears only once in all the writings of Tertullian. Perhaps Trench is correct when he surmises that the word was "so steeped in heathenism, so linked with profane associations, and desecrated by them . . . that the early Christians shrank instinctively from the word."

The final word is *ōdē*. It is the most general word of the three. It is a generic word which may apply to any kind of song. For this reason it is qualified by the word "spiritual" in order to separate it from secular music. This is the word used for the "song of Moses" and the "song of the lamb" (Rev. 15:3) and the "new song" of Revelation 5:9 and 14:3.

What then can be said about the differences between "psalms, hymns, and spiritual songs"? The psalm is like the Psalm of the Old Testament: the words of Scripture put to music and sung with instrumental accompaniment. Some would call it an anthem. The hymn is any song of praise to God the Father, the Son, or the Holy Spirit. In fact, the Roman historian, Pliny reported that the Christians made a habit of singing hymns to Christ as to God (*Letters* 10. 96). "Spiritual songs," it seems, refers to all types of music not covered specifically by the first two terms. In particular, the term probably refers to or, at the least, includes the simple music of the common man, in contrast to the higher form of the psalm.

In any case what should be noted is that the early church was a singing church and, contrary to the belief of a few modern groups, the early believers used instruments to accompany their singing. In addition, they used a variety of songs, from the complicated anthem to the two- or three-chord spiritual songs. Because of this they were able to minister to everyone from the common layman to the most accomplished musician.

60

Forbearance

Twice in the Epistle to the Romans the Apostle Paul speaks about the "forbearance" of God. He asks the Jews, "Or despisest thou the riches of his goodness and forbearance and longsuffering ...?" (Rom. 2:4). Again, he writes, "To declare his righteousness for the remission of sins that are past, through the forbearance of God" (Rom. 3:25 b). The word for "forbearance" is *anochē* which means "a holding back" or "a delay" of punishment.

In classical Greek, it signified a truce or a stopping of hostilities. The verb form of the word (*anochē*) was used in the Greek papyri to describe the expiration of a statute of limitations. It was used by the Stoics in one of their formulae concerning how to deal with different kinds of people: "Put up with the one and take advantage of the other" (Moulton and Milligan).

In Romans 2:4 *anochē* is used with the word "longsuffering" (*makrothumia*). Some have understood these to mean the same thing, with the difference being only one of degree. However, *anoche* is temporary, and like a truce it will pass away after a certain period of time unless a new agreement is made. On the other hand, longsuffering, while it is similar, does not imply any time limit—it could conceivably go on forever. In the Romans passages *anochē* describes "that truce with the sinner, which by no means implies that the wrath will not be executed at the last; nay, involves that it certainly will, unless he be found under new conditions of repentance and obedience" (Trench).

The verb form, *anechō,* is used fourteen times in the New

144

Testament. Jesus utilizes it with the same sense that the noun form has in Matthew 17:17; "How long shall I suffer you?" It means "to put up with," "bear with," or "endure." The believer is to endure persecution and tribulation because he knows that these are only temporary and will soon pass (1 Cor. 4:12; 2 Thess. 1:4). The believer is to "suffer the word of exhortation," even though sometimes it may not be pleasant because it is for his good (Heb. 13:22); yet he is to realize that the insincere will not "endure sound doctrine" (2 Tim. 4:3).

Believers are to put up with one another in love in order to achieve unity in the body (Eph. 4:2; Col. 3:13). On the other hand, the believer is not to "forbear" the wrong people such as the false teachers who opposed the Apostle Paul (2 Cor. 11:4,19,20). There is such a thing as being too tolerant of error because it is the easiest course to follow.

One must conclude that discernment is needed to know with whom one is to "forbear" (put up with) and how long one is to forbear (since *anochē* implies a limited amount of time). To have this discernment, one must depend on the directions in the Scriptures and the guidance of the Holy Spirit.

61

Whatsoever Things are Pure

In Philippians 4:8 the Apostle Paul presents a list of virtuous and praiseworthy qualities, and gives a command for the believer to "think on these things." Ralph Martin, in his *New Century Bible Commentary* on Philippians, states that this means more than merely "keeping in mind" these things, but even making these things "the *logos* of your personal universe."[18] One should meditate on these things and allow them to shape his conduct.

Some of the things on which we are to think continually are "whatsoever things are pure." The word for "pure" in this passage is *hagnos*. This word may have a wide range of meaning, just as our word "pure" may have. Originally, it meant "in a condition prepared for worship" (Moulton and Milligan). It was also applied to things dedicated to God, such as offerings or places of worship (holy places). It meant pure from defilement, not contaminated.

Another application which it had in classical Greek times was in reference to the Greek gods. It was used to describe several of them, but it was primarily referring to Artemis, the virgin goddess. By this use it came to mean "pure" in the sense of chaste and was applied to young maidens. In a more general sense it came to mean guiltless and upright (Liddell and Scott).

In the Greek Old Testament it refers only to ceremonial purification. Joshua challenged the people of Israel, "Purify yourselves: for tomorrow the Lord will do wonders among you" (Josh. 3:5). In the New Testament the verb form of *hagnos* occurs only seven times, four of these also referring to ceremonial purity. John speaks of the Jew's purifying themselves for the Passover (John 11:55). Acts also employs the word in relation to purification in preparation for taking a vow (Acts 21:24,26, 24:18). In one case *hagnos* refers to more purification in general or freedom from every fault. "And every man that hath this hope in him purifieth himself, even as he is pure" (1 John 3:3).

In at least four instances *hagnos* refers to moral purity (2 Cor. 11:2; 1 Tim. 5:22; Titus 2:5; 1 Peter 3:2). The most striking of these is found in 2 Corinthians 11:2. Paul says, "For I am jealous over you with godly jealousy: for I have espoused you to one husband, that I may present you as a chaste virgin to Christ." So in its strictest moral usage it refers not only to chastity, but to virginity.

The believer is to concentrate his thoughts on both ceremonial, as well as moral purity, and everything related to purity. In addition to *hagnos* two other words have basic meaning related to the concept of purity. One of these is *eilikrines.* It occurs only twice in the New Testament. Paul prays for the Philippians that they may be "pure and without offense until the day of Christ" (Phil. 1:10). Peter speaks of the "pure minds" of his readers (2 Peter 3:1). There are two opinions concerning the etymology of *eilikrines.* The more probable is that the term comes from a combination of words meaning "that which is cleansed by much rolling and shaking to and fro in the seive" (Trench). Others, however, favor the view that the most words refer to that which is "held up to the sunlight," and thereby tested and shown to be pure. Trench argues for the first idea by saying, "It is not so much the clear, the transparent, as the purged, the winnowed, the unmingled" (Trench). The kindred word *elikrineia* is used in 1 Corinthians 5:8 with the idea of "purging out" the old leaven, which lends support to the idea of removing the impure. From this root meaning it came to mean moral purity in New Testament times.

The final word which is translated "pure" is *katharos.* More often it is translated by the English word "clean." In the Greek poets it was used concerning one who was physically clean or was wearing clean clothing. It also meant pure in the sense of being free from any admixture of a foreign substance. It is used of water, bread, grain, and metals. Morally, it can refer to freedom from guilt, and ceremonially, it denotes one who is fit to approach or serve God. In the later Greek papyri, several interesting uses have also been found. *Katharos* is used to describe an animal that is without blemish, a document which is free from errors, and a person who is ready to enter the temple.

In the New Testament *kathros* is used in three different ways, first to describe physical cleanness. Matthew writes that the body of Jesus was wrapped in a clean cloth (Matt. 27:59). It also describes the clothing worn by the bride of Christ (Rev. 19:8) and the armies of heaven (Rev. 19:14). Next, it is used in the Levitical or ceremonial sense. Speaking of food, the Apostle Paul stresses that all things are *katharos* (Rom. 14:20). Finally, its most relevant use for this discussion is ethical. Titus 1:15 says, "To the pure all things are pure." Paul tells Timothy to have "love out of a pure heart and a good conscience (1 Tim. 1:5). Again he reminds him to flee "youthful lusts: but follow righteousness, faith, charity, peace, with them that call on the Lord out of a pure heart" (2 Tim. 2:22)—(see also 1 Tim. 3:9 and 2 Tim. 1:3.)

In its ethical sense, *katharos* means pure, "contemplated under the aspect of the clean, the freedom from soil or stain" (Trench). *Eilikrines* is the word which describes the believer when every factor which would divide his heart and cause him to be double-minded has been removed. He will have a "pure mind."

Finally, *hagnos* describes the person who has kept himself pure and undefiled in body. He is chaste and free from the ravages of carnal living. God desires that we be pure in every aspect. "Whatsoever things are pure . . . think on these things."

62

Whatsoever Things
are Lovely

In Philippians 4:8 the "Christian moral ideal" is presented. "It embraces practically all that was of value in ancient ethics" (*Expositor's Greek Testament*). J. B. Lightfoot commented that the first four words (true, honest, just, and pure) describe the character of the actions themselves; the fifth and sixth words (lovely and of good report) point to the moral approval which they bring into effect. (The words "just" and "pure" have been discussed previously).

The word for "lovely" is *prosphilēs* which means "pleasing, agreeable." It is a combination of *pros* (toward) and *phileō* (to love); therefore, it literally refers to things in the direction of love or things leading to love. In fact, the verb form often means "to approach so as to kiss."

Prosphilēs is a rarely-used word; it occurs only here in the New Testament. It was used in secular Greek to describe persons who are dear, beloved, friendly, kindly affectioned, or well-disposed (Liddell and Scott). In a letter written in 121 AD, Plotina, the wife of the Roman Emperor Trajan, used the verb form of the word in reference to Trajan's successor. It was also used commonly in epitaphs.

A second appropriation of the word is to describe things which are lovely or pleasing. In one papyrus, the word described a temple which had recently been completed. The most important use, however, was in describing actions as lovely. This last use is found in Philippians 4:8. We are to contemplate the kind of behavior which is lovely and pleasing in the sight of God. *Prosphilēs,* then, does not describe a particular virtue, such as truth, honor, righteousness, or purity, but it points to actions as they are viewed by God. Let us then desire to do "whatsoever" is "lovely" to Him.

63

Things of Good Report

The sixth item in Philippians 4:8 on which we are to center our thoughts is *euphēmos* (a person or thing of good report). It is a combination of *eu* (well, good) and *phēmē* (report). It is an extremely rare word and occurs only once in the New Testament.

In classical Greek it meant uttering sounds of good omen, referred to the keeping of a holy silence (especially before a prayer), and alluded to fairsounding speech (see Liddell and Scott). A kindred word, *euphēmia,* is also used once in the New Testament in 2 Corinthians 6:8: "Through glory and dishonour, through ill report and good report." This word also means a silence before a prayer.

In addition, it denoted prayer or praise offered in worship to the Greek gods, a fair or honorable name for a bad thing (euphemism). The sense in which Paul uses the word in 2 Corinthians 6:8 is also found in secular literature. It means a good reputation enjoyed by a man. Paul declared he would continue to serve God whether people said good or bad things about him.

What then is the difference between *euphēmia* and *euphēmos?* Do they mean the same thing? Or is there a difference in emphasis? Lightfoot argues that *euphēmos* in Philippians 4:8 does not mean " 'well-spoken of, well reputed,' for the word seems never to have this passive meaning; but with its usual active sense, 'fair-speaking,' and so 'winning, attractive.' " The evidence from the papyri seem to agree with that conclusion.

Euphēmia seems to denote one's reputation, although it is

used sometimes in reference to one's speech and how it sounds. *Euphēmos,* on the other hand, primarily refers to what one says. It "signifies the delicacy which guards the lips, that nothing may be expressed in public worship that could disturb devotion or give rise to scandal" (see Moulton and Milligan).

When Paul says to think on "whatsoever things are of good report" he means to consider carefully what you are going to speak before you say it. He refers to "things spoken in a kindly spirit, with good-will to others" (Thayer).

FOOTNOTES

1 William Barclay, *New Testament Words,* Philadelphia: The Westminster Press, 1964, p. 86.

2 *Ibid.,* p. 175.

3 William Barclay, *The Letters To The Corinthians,* in *The Daily Study Bible,* 17 Vols., Edinburgh: The Saint Andrew Press, 1954, p. 121

4 William Barclay, *The Letters to The Philippians, Colossians and Thessalonians,* in *The Daily Study Bible,* 17 Vols., Edinburgh: The Saint Andrew Press, 1954, p. 189.

5 *Ibid.,* p. 18.

6 *Ibid.,* p. 17.

7 William Barclay, *New Testament Words,* Philadelphia: The Westminster Press, 1964, p. 277.

8 *Ibid.,* p. 280.

9 *Ibid.,* p. 223.

10 *Ibid.,* p. 224.

11 William Barclay, *The Letters to the Galations and Ephesians,* in *The Daily Study Bible,* 17 Vols., Edinburgh: The Saint Andrew Press, 1954, p. 53.

12 William Barclay, *The Letters to the Philippians, Colossians and Thessalonians,* in *The Daily Study Bible,* 17 Vols., Edinburgh: The Saint Andrew Press, 1954, p. 21.

13 William Barclay, *New Testament Words,* Philadelphia: The Westminster Press, 1964, p. 143.

14 *Ibid.,* p. 145.

15 William Barclay, *The Letters to the Corinthians,* in *The Daily Study Bible,* 17 Vols., Edinburgh: The Saint Andrew Press, 1954, p. 262.

16 William Barclay, *New Testament Words,* Philadelphia: The Westminster Press, 1964, p. 125.

17 *Ibid.,* p. 95.

18 Ralph Martin, *Philippians,* in *The New Century Bible Commentary,* Grand Rapids: William B. Eerdmans Publishing Co., 1980, p. 157.

SELECTED REFERENCES

Barclay, William. *New Testament Words.* Philadelphia: The West-minster Press, 1964.

_____. *The Daily Study Bible.* 17 Vols. Edinburgh: The Saint Andrew Press, 1954.

Bauer, Walter. *A Greek-English Lexicon of the New Testament and Other Early Christian Literature.* Fourth ed. Translated and edited by William F. Arndt and F. Wilbur Gingrich. Chicago: University of Chicago Press, 1952.

Lightfoot, J.B. *St Paul's Epistles to the Colossians and to Philemon.* Grand Rapids: Zondervan Publishing House, reprint of the 1879 edition, 1976.

_____. *St. Paul's Epistle to the Philippians.* London: Macmillan and Company, 1913.

Milligan, George. *Selections from the Greek Papyri.* Freeport, N.Y.: Books for Libraries Press, reprint of the 1910 edition, 1969.

Moulton, James Hope and George Milligan. *The Vocabulary of The Greek New Testament.* Grand Rapids: Wm. B. Eerdmans Publishing Company, reprint of the 1930 edition, 1982.

Nicoll, W. Robertson, editor. *The Expositor's Greek Testament.* 5 Vols. Grand Rapids: Wm. B. Eerdmans, reprint, 1974.

Robertson, A.T. *Word Pictures in the New Testament.* 6 Vols. Nashville: Broadman Press, 1931.

Thayer, Joseph Henry. *A Greek-English Lexicon of the New Testament* Edinburgh: T. and T. Clark, 4th ed., 1901.

Trench, Richard C. *Synonyms of the New Testament.* Grand Rapids: Wm. B. Eerdmans Publishing Company, reprint of the 1880 ed., 1975.

Vine. W.E. *Vine's Expository Dictionary of New Testament Words.* McLean, Virginia: MacDonald Publishing Company, 1939.

Wuest, Kenneth S. *Wuest's Word Studies.* 4 Vols. Grand Rapids: Wm. B. Eerdmans Publishing Company, reprint, 1978.

INDEX OF NEW TESTAMENT REFERENCES

155

156 SERMON STARTERS FROM THE GREEK NEW TESTAMENT

17:9 17   2:19 137,138   11:24 79
18:34 130   2:22 136,137   11:26 48,49
19:42 13   2:38 64-67,89   13:2 124
21:7 138   2:41 89   13:9 78
22:63 117   2:42 28   13:24 65
23:11 117   2:43 137   13:33 142
23:16,22 36   3:21 19   13:45 86
23:35 116   4:8 78   13:52 78
23:36 117   4:12 127   14:3 137
23:43 66   4:29 21   14:26 18
23:47 96   4:30 137   15:5 100
24:44 142   4:31 78   15:12 137
John 1:1 131   5:11 60   15:15 128
1:29 24   5:12 137   15:19 59
2:3 76   5:13,36 34   15:20,29 81
2:5,9 54   5:17 86,100   15:28 109
2:17 86   5:41 71   16:15,33 89
2:29 95   6:1-71 55   16:31 118
3:15 118   6:3 78   17:32 116
3:16 39   6:5 79   17:34 34
3:34 131   6:8 137   18:8 89
4:35-38 125,127   6:10 42   19:4 65
4:48 137   7:22 36   19:5 89
4:54 138   7:36 137   19:32,39,41...........60
8:15 58   7:38 60   19:38 128
8:34 21   7:46 17   20:17,28 56
8:46 24   7:52 95   20:24 128
10:21 85   7:55 79   20:31 37
10:41 138   7:60 24   20:35 125
11:5 39   8:1 60   21:24 147
11:55 147   8:12,13,16,36-38....89   21:26 147
12:2 54   8:22 63   22:16 89,90
12:48 58   8:29 34   23:6 73
13:34 40   9:17 78   24:2 13
14:21 39   9:18 89   24:4 134
17:26 39   9:26 34   24:5 100
20:27 119   10:22 48   24:14 50,101
20:30 138   10:28 34   24:18 147
21:15-17 41   10:29 128   26:5 100
Acts 1:1 128   10:36 13   26:6,7 73
1:3 72   10:37 130   26:20 63
1:14 15   10:43 66   26:28 49
2:4 78   10:46 66   28:20 73
2:13 75,116   10:47,48 89   28:22 100
```
```